The Next Horizon

"LE MORAN TAING"
EOGHANN
E. Nicholson

Memories of a
Hebridean Skipper

by
Ewen Nicholson,
with Allan Henderson

1

Contents

'God grant me the serenity
To accept the things I cannot change ;
Courage to change the things I can;
And wisdom to know the difference.'

Reinhold Niebuhr

Preface

There is a certain belief that everyone has a story to tell. Ewen Nicholson is proof of that. Blessed with a natural Hebridean flare for storytelling, he has retained much of the lore imparted to him as a child, and continues to delight in the meeting of others and sharing of stories, being a champion of that rarest of beasts, conversation.

There was nothing unusual about Ewen Nicholson's upbringing. His is an experience shared with thousands of other Hebrideans of a similar age; the familiar cycle of life on a croft, the back breaking labour in support of one's community and family.

Neither was his education in any way out of the ordinary. Nothing more than a brief stepping stone to the role of bread winner, for all but those that showed a serious academic bent.

His decision to forge a career in the Merchant Navy was hardly unorthodox, during an era when virtually every ship sailing under the 'red duster' counted at least a sprinkling of islanders or boys from the western seaboard among their crews.

What separates Ewen Nicholson from his peers, is the diversity of experience he has known, and an almost photo like recollection of every road his life has taken, and there have been many. From farm hand to radio operator, navvie to lobster fisherman, and all stations in between. He has witnessed war and mutiny and lived to tell the tale.

There exists within Scotland's Gaels a need to wander, a nomadic gene, as it were. Hardly a corner of the globe has not been touched by their presence at some time or other. During his time at sea, Ewen Nicholson visited every continent, sampling many cultures, often acting as emissary between those at home in the islands and the myriad displaced of the great Celtic diaspora.

We are afforded, through this memoir, a perspective of life on an isolated Hebridean island. Survival was clearly paramount, and one is left with the impression of a family prepared for the battle, readied for all that life will throw at them by a strong and, at times, domineering patriarchal figure. Indeed, it could be said that Ewen has inherited a lot of his father's characteristics. Fiercely independent, headstrong, forthright and stubborn to a fault, but with a natural inclination to help his fellow man (the latter possibly a product of his unshakeable Christian faith).

My father tending a ewe with triplets and, if you look carefully, my mother filling a pail from the peat stack.

He has always proved adept at adjusting to his surroundings as required. The remoteness of the Uists, the big city modernity of Glasgow and New York, the colour of revolutionary Cuba. All have been negotiated with equal relish. Ewen Nicholson has lived many lives and has survived

6

many close shaves with an almost feline persistence. His has been, as the locution would have it, 'a hard old paper round,' and this book is all the better for it.

Most importantly, this is a story of one man's victory over his demons. Ewen Nicholson is not a wealthy man, not for him the trappings of fame or fortune. Yet he has found an inner contentment, reconciled with his past and ready for his future. For him, retirement is anathema. He has his health and strength and for that he is grateful. The 'Grimsay Isle' ploughs a steady course through the waters of Scotland's west coast, and still yet, the wonder of what might be just across the horizon.

A young Ewen flanked by brother Angus and sister Ann

Living on an Island

My name is Ewen Alexander Nicholson.

I was born on July 19th 1935, to Andrew and Margaret Nicholson of 'Taigh a Bhàigh', Grimsay, North Uist. My parents were both from Grimsay. My father's people, long ago, came from Bracadale in Skye, and if we go back far enough, they were probably Norse people, as I have discovered that there are ten or eleven ways to spell Nicholson, in various different languages including Norwegian and Russian. My mother was a MacLean, and she took great pride in telling us that she was of the MacLeans of Boreray. Somebody still has a book, which shows that clan going back to the 12th or 13th century.

My father's mother was a MacDiarmid. They were quite famous too. I'm proud that I still have a photo of some of my grandmother's family before they emigrated to the Carolinas. The Macaulays on my mother's side, they were a bit laid back, but they also emigrated, this time to New Zealand and Australia. My father also used to speak of a relative called Angus MacLean, who went 'deep sea' under sail at that time. He did very well and ended up having the pilotage of the Clyde, the Mersey and the Thames, which was quite an honour. My dad could recall, as a young lad, watching Angus docking his ship at 'KG5' in Glasgow, walking from side to side on the bridge of a boat called the 'Baharrista'. He was also supposed to have been in charge of a ship that was carrying the treasures of the King of Persia over to America for safekeeping. Who knows if that was true or not? My father was also very proud of our family connection to the heroine of the 1745 Jacobite uprising, Flora MacDonald.

I have a photograph on the wall of my family home, and I was showing it recently to some friends from Glasgow. They said to me, "weren't you lucky in them days. We were all in a

9

single end." I suppose it made me feel quite proud that we had what was probably quite a big bungalow at that time.

I am the oldest of eight children. There were four boys and four girls. Angus after me, then Ann, then Margaret, then Effie, followed by Morag, my brother John, who died tragically young of cancer at the age of twenty-seven, and then my youngest brother Archie, who was sadly drowned in a diving accident two years ago.

A grown Up Ewen with little brother Archie in 1959.

Times were hard in the 1930s, especially in the big cities, as people coped with the aftermath of the Great War and the collapse of the stock markets in both London and New York. Life on a Hebridean island was very hard going indeed, though most of us became good workers from a very early age, something which was definitely encouraged and instilled in us by my father. I've a sneaky feeling that people long ago had big families for cheap labour.

We depended on food that we caught, hunted and grew. Fish, like flounders, were caught on great hand lines, which held up to five hundred hooks, or were speared in tidal pools with a hay fork. Rabbits were snared or shot with a gun, which could equally be turned to good use on sea birds. Even the odd sea trout would find its way into the family pot.

When I look back, I always think of people then being very friendly and helpful, sometimes sharing their food, and always sharing the labour of the seasonal work like ploughing, sheep shearing and peat cutting. This help was usually given on a barter basis, as money was very short. It certainly wasn't prudent to fall out with your neighbour, as you never knew when you would be glad of their help.

Grimsay was a tidal island up until the early sixties. This meant that all movement depended on the state of the tides. When the tide was out you crossed the fords either on foot or by horse and cart, and, if you could afford it, you hired a gig, which could take up to six passengers. When the tide was in, you used a boat powered by engine, oars or sail. My uncle Alexander had the post office, (which is still run by my cousin Ewen), and he relied on the mail coming on horseback, boat and tractor, via Carinish, from Lochmaddy. Years ago there was also a mail boat which came to Leirinish in Uist from Dunvegan in Skye. 'Seonaidh Mhurchaidh', who lived with his family at Carinish, collected the mails and also did the run to Grimsay and Benbecula. We were also used to cargo vessels coming into Ceallan harbour on Grimsay. These were run by 'MacCallum Orm' and, latterly, 'MacBraynes', so we weren't quite as isolated as people may imagine. The Macleans of Boreray built a very good road over a hundred years ago on the north side of Grimsay to their main steading and home at Leac na Sìth, Ceallan, then, before the outbreak of the second war, a gravel foot path was constructed which circled the island. This made travel a lot easier, especially for the postman, who delivered either on foot or by horse with pouches slung over the horse's back.

11

Our local postman at that time, Ewen Campbell, was quite a character, but he also had a very short fuse. He would have saddle bags on Paddy the horse, which, during the war, were invariably full of dried milk for babies and so on. In a fit of temper one day he told a local that the men of Grimsay should be marrying more buxom women who were more able to produce their own milk, so as to reduce his work load and the weight in his poor horse's saddle bags!

Horses were very much a part of everyday life. Ewen Campbell would take Paddy the horse to get shoed at the smith in Nunton, Benbecula. On one particular occasion, Paddy managed to eject Ewen in the middle of Oitir Mhòr, and galloped home to Grimsay without getting his new shoes. His master had to walk home none too pleased, having to take his shoes off to wade the ford. Most ironic don't you think.

Another of our postmen, Archie MacDonald, had become something of a celebrity after escaping over the Pyrenees from the Germans during the Second World War. He had been taken prisoner with the 51st Highland Division at St. Valery, escaped and made his way to freedom after bamboozling guards at a German checkpoint by speaking Gaelic to them. They had no idea where he was from, and let him go.

There were several shops around Grimsay at that time. The Isle of Flodda and Gramsdale both had two, and Carinish had two and a post office. My father had a small butcher's shop and usually butchered three sheep weekly. Very occasionally, he would also butcher a bull or a cow. As young children, we delivered the parcels of mutton or beef, carrying them on our backs all over the island, and, on occasion, to Cnoc Cuidhein and Claddach Carinish. Some of our customers enjoyed mealy puddings, so we would clean and deliver the 'Mudal Mhor' and various other bits of offal including the head. One job I detested was skinning and singeing the sheep's head, which I would carry out on my return from school. The head was considered a delicacy, especially the brain, eyes and tongue. Nothing was wasted. The skin was also dried and made into lovely bedside rugs.

We had about twenty sheep of our own, but most of the slaughtered animals were bought locally from Eval hill and the island of Rona. Father also had some sheep on good grazing on the Monach islands. He would buy a number of three year old wedders, which, when slaughtered, could weigh up to sixty pounds. In those days the humane gun was not compulsory and I used to feel so sorry for those poor animals having their throats cut.

Our croft was seventeen acres, of which about six was arable. We were allowed twenty sheep and followers, two cows and followers and one horse. This was called 'souming' under the old crofting laws. As a crofter, you also had a share in the common grazing, which, in our case, consisted of an apportionment on the Grimsay moor and many of the numerous small islands nearby; Eilean nan Laogh, Eilean na Dairbe, Eilean Mòr, Eilean Beag and countless others. I can remember giving my father a hand to line our boat with bracken so that the beasts wouldn't damage themselves, and I've seen him taking as many as eight or nine stircs and putting them ashore on Rona.

I have always been interested in the names of those islands, which are undoubtedly clues to our ancient history. For example, near our family home, there was an island 'Eilean Mhic Crath' (MacRae's Island), so it is a fair assumption that a man of that name had some connection with the place once. Our Scottish Ordnance Survey maps are full of lovely names that are absolutely soaked in our heritage and culture. I remember in primary school a boy was asked by the teacher to name an island off the west coast of Scotland. He quickly blurted out "Eilean a' Gheòidh", which is in fact very small, being only two hundred yards round its coastline.

As a small boy I remember herding the township cattle and sheep during the spring and summer time. In those days, over sixty years ago, the crofters built stone dykes round their crofts to keep other people's stock out and their own in. We used to herd the cattle onto the small tidal island of 'Eilean na H-Airidh' so that when the tide came in, it would also act as a barrier. This didn't always work, as there was often the odd beast that would swim back to their croft to get at the corn.

Crofting was hard. When subsidies became available it lightened our financial burden, but it certainly did nothing to decrease the amount of manual labour required to run a croft properly. Prior to the heavy rainfalls of winter, we had to dig and clean all the drains that, in our case, flowed into the sea. Then we would collect 'Shibidh' (blown seaweed) which would be forked ashore to make compost for the vegetable patch or for making 'lazy beds', which I have always considered a strange name, as they require such hard work to construct and maintain. To begin with, you measured out the ground with a string and spade so that the beds were uniform. Then you spread seaweed on them to a depth of about six inches, which was left exposed to the elements for a few weeks before being turned with a spade.

After that, a trench, about a foot wide, was constructed on either side of the seaweed that you had previously laid. The soil from the trenches was used to fill in the centre of the lazy bed (or feannagan as we called them locally), which became raised and used for planting crops.

A few weeks later, planting would begin in earnest using an implement called a dibble. The seed potatoes would be carefully selected and planted six inches apart. These were then covered with soil using a special wooden rake for the job. Even the seaweed for the potato patch was specially selected, being cut near the low spring tide mark with a sickle, which had to be sharpened every so often with a special stone. Just before the tide was on the turn, we encircled the amount we had cut and secured it with manila rope. Then, when the tide was at the correct height, we towed it home behind our boat.

14

Sometimes we also used a horse and cart or a sledge called a 'Lusgin' to carry this fertiliser to the croft.

The month of March was often used to begin the whole operation and we would begin to dig the potatoes around July, with an implement called a 'cròcan'. If the return was in the region of six sacks to one planted, we were happy enough. The same ground was then left fallow for two or more years while crop rotation was exercised.

Back in those days, my dad would cut huge sods of turf and use them to construct what we called a 'Torr' for the potatoes. This was specially built with space for air to circulate, and carefully filled with hay or straw during the frosty weather. The top of this construction was roofed with specially cut 'sgrathan' or sods, and roped and pegged to make it weatherproof. If we had space in the barn, we would also put some potatoes in there, although this meant that you had to run the gauntlet of rats, which weren't our only worry, as some years much of the crop would be lost to blight. This was a serious business, as the potato was a mainstay of our diet back then, sometimes eaten twice a day on their own, or with fish, or a glass of milk. The varieties were so familiar to me; 'Champion', 'Edzell Blue' and 'Maris Piper'.

My earliest years were carefree times, although as you have read, for my parents and the other grownups around me, survival on an island like Grimsay was an unrelenting battle. Soon enough though, it was time for me to take my first steps on the road to adulthood, when I attended Grimsay Primary School.

An Island Education

I was about five and a half when I first went to school. This involved a walk of about a mile over bogs and hills, which didn't do me any harm at all. There were probably in the region of about thirty children in the school at this time, and it was simply known as Grimsay Public School.

I well remember my first day. My father took me to a place called the 'Athan' at the end of our croft, where I crossed over the stone causeway to 'Cnoc na h-Àirigh Chèir'. It was there that I was met by our neighbour, Archie MacLean, who took me the rest of the way to the school.

The school had one room, with an old curtain dividing the younger children from the older ones. My father was a county councillor at the time, and he arranged for the director of education to pay us a visit, so that he could see the state of the place. On the day of the visit, the director approached the curtain; and my father shook it, covering the director in soot and dust. Soon after, we were given a proper wooden partition. The education authorities had obviously got the message.

There were usually two teachers in the school, my first being Kenneth MacLeod. My Aunty also taught me for a while, although I had to refer to her as Mrs Nicholson just like everyone else. After that we had Kate Nicholson, from Skye, who was married to my cousin, and John MacAskill, my first cousin from Newton Ferry, so my education became something of a family affair. I also recall Miss MacDougal, from Bayhead, and Miss MacCorkindale, from Carinish. I have mostly fond memories of my teachers. However, I wasn't above playing tricks on them. We had one teacher called Donald MacLennan, who became known as 'Donald Duck'. Little did I know that I would end up, later in life, with a Doctor Donald Duck in Mallaig. Anyway, I hid the belt from him one day, and when he eventually found it, it was in the school oven, as hard as a brick. Imagine my horror when the whereabouts of the belt was discovered, and, worse still, realizing that I was in line to be strapped with the now extra hard piece of leather. However, 'Ewen' was not to be deterred. I rolled the belt up, neatly placing it in an empty can of syrup, and pressed down the lid. Inside the watertight container I placed a carefully written poem, the meaning of which has always fascinated me. It read as follows;

'Down at the bottom of the deep, blue sea
Thrashing fish for Donald's tea.'

We often hid or otherwise disposed of the infamous strap, so that our poor teacher, Mr. MacLennan, had to buy luggage type straps from my uncle Alec at 'Gob an Rubha' post office and shop.

We were certainly no angels. The ruler we had been given was put to good use sending chewed up blotting paper missiles to the roof of the classroom, or, worse still, at one another. Another favourite prank was sending notes to each other. If the note was of an offensive nature, it would be eaten quickly by the recipient, before the fast approaching teacher could read it.

The Head Teacher had a long leather strap with three prongs, which, in my day, was used quite often. We sometimes nicked these prongs with a penknife, so that as soon as someone was strapped, the prongs would fly off, much to the relief of the pupil and the rage of the teacher.

The day in school always started with prayers, followed by catechism, and then the school roll was taken. Truancy was rare. I recall a friend and I played this dodge once, and felt the day much longer than if we had been to school. Worse was to follow though, as one of the girls reported me to my parents, and my Dad belted me much harder than any schoolmaster would have done.

We sat at small wooden desks, which had a compartment for books, a receptacle for ink, and were equipped with a pencil, a pen, a rubber, blotting paper, crayons, plasticine, a ruler and a copy-book, which proved to be a most effective method of learning to write. We used old-fashioned pens with a nib and ink, so that the blotting paper was never too far away either. I think people's hand-writing was much more legible in those days. It seemed to deteriorate after the invention of the biro. We were also issued with a slate that we wrote on using the crayons or a slate pencil. The teacher, of course, had a larger version of this mounted on an easel. As a young boy, my father had a teacher who was nicknamed 'Foinnean' (Warty). One day, my father drew a likeness of 'Foinnean' on the blackboard. When the teacher discovered this, he made my father stand in front of the class holding his attempt at art, with the following credentials; 'A BORN ARTIST, YOU FOOL!' How times change.

At school we were blessed to have lovely, clean sands to play on. When the tide was in, we played with toy wooden boats that we had made ourselves, the sea never being far from our thoughts as young boys. There were two breaks per day called 'Am Pleidh Mòr' and 'Am Pleidh Beag'. The first one in the morning lasted about twenty minutes, and we played games like 'Yenders', skipping, 'Evie, Ovie' and 'Hide and Seek'. We would also have a tug of war if someone could get their hands on a bit of rope or 'Ciadh' or 'Ropa Ruadh' as we called it. Us boys would also go off to nearby islands to build piers and small sheilings. I can still hear Mr. MacLennan frantically blowing on his whistle to call us back to work. Occasionally, we would ignore this, getting the belt for our act of disobedience.

The main school break was for lunch. Some of us went home, while others brought pieces with cheese, margarine or sometimes crowdie. We also had girdle scones and oatcakes. The school would issue us with cocoa, horlicks and dried milk made with water and heated on the stove.

We used to love sledging during the winter. We didn't get all that much snow, but certainly more than we do today. Your

18

first task was always to find a herring barrel, which could be split into staves. Next you took three or four of these staves and fixed them together to form a kind of oval sledge. It worked a treat. Another thing we enjoyed, which was also quite dangerous, involved obtaining a rubber tyre, say off a lorry, climbing inside it and rolling down a hill.

As with all the other local families, Gaelic was our first language in the house. I only had two words of English when I went to school, 'yes' and 'no'. This meant, in common with all the other children, that English had to be learned at school. There were one or two children who came to the school during the war that didn't have Gaelic, but, by and large, everyone did. It was strange because inside the classroom, all our lessons were conducted in English, whereas outside, at play times and outwith school, we always communicated in our first language, Gaelic. It all seemed to work fine.

When all is said and done, school days were fun, and if I got belted, then I probably deserved it. Those small, rural schools produced many a good scholar. There are many examples of this; William Shepherd Morrison, from a place called Ruchdaidh, near Trombaisgearraidh, who became speaker of the House of Commons and the one time Governor General of Australia; my cousin Angus MacLean Master Mariner, who, as you read earlier, had the pilotage of the Clyde, the Mersey and the Thames. My late uncle John Nicholson was educated in the same school, and was a surgeon in Palestine and Egypt during the first war. Soldiers used to come to him complaining of sand in their eyes, and sometimes, if busy, he would send them off with the remark, "So have I!"

The school building is still standing and can be seen near the lovely stretch of sand in Grimsay. It is no longer a school and has been bought by my cousin who lives in England. The building is a good example of real craftsmanship. The stone work is a work of art compared to the concrete blocks they use today. It's incredible to think that many of these old school

19

buildings (which still survive) were built around 1850. That may have been when education became compulsory.

From the month of March until October we would go to school barefoot. We used to have a contest to see who would be first to put their boots on when the cold weather returned. Although our parents would try and ensure that we left the house with boots on during the winter months, these were quickly removed and hidden on the way to school if there was a competition involved. Back in those days you were lucky to own one pair of boots, which often had tackets or metal plates on the soles. Woe betide you if you kicked stones with these on, as the front of the boot would show tell tale signs, and then you would show tell tale signs of a leathering on your rear end. My dad was quite good at repairing boots, and had a cobbler's last, as most houses had at that time. My cousin, Donald Alec Ruadh, learned the trade of cobbler in Australia, and if there was a big complicated repair needed, we would take the foot wear to him at Bagh Mòr.

After school in the afternoon, there were countless jobs to be done around the croft, with animals and fowls to be cared for. The hens, chickens, ducks, geese, turkeys and any others had to be fed and cared for. I never liked it when it was my turn to clean out the hen house, although, as a family, we became very adept at rearing and developing our feathered friends. At one time we had twenty geese and one or two ganders, which were most productive, the goose egg being the size of four hens' eggs. The only problem with the geese was the mess they made of the corn, trampling all over it when the grain appeared, making it very difficult to scythe. We had to keep the hens out of the corn as well, and we would build a sheiling on a nearby islet to keep them in while it was ripening.   They still had to be fed twice a day of course, and if the tide was in, we would row over in a small cobble, which at one time belonged to the late Mr. Beveridge from Valley. As children we became very used to taking this craft on small trips, getting us used to the sea. From the age of about seven, I was quite capable of handling her in all conditions, and was becoming quite used to the currents, the weather and so on.

My father would sometimes hatch out mallard duck eggs, which had been wrapped in wool and placed under the victoress stove. He was very good with animals. With a bit of care and attention they would eventually hatch, and we would then let them roam around with the other ducks. They seemed to get on fine with their domestic cousins. On one occasion he put a double yolk egg under a broody hen and a chicken with four legs was hatched. This, of course, should not have been attempted as the hen shunned the chicken and eventually killed the poor creature. On a croft, you learn very early on that nature is cruel. It was good to get fresh eggs everyday, and I mean fresh, with yolks bright red, as the hens were so near the sea, and scratched about in the seaweed picking up a lot of lime which gave the yolks their colour and kept their shells strong. It is an amazing thing when you consider that the 'Creator' has shaped a hen's egg in such a way that it offers just the right amount of protection. Any other shape would end in disaster. At one time we had an old boat turned upside down and this worked perfectly as a hen house. We installed rafters for the hens to perch on and installed boxes for them to lay their eggs in. There was also straw on the floor, which was changed every so often.

I can remember sometimes waiting for a hen to lay, as we would be short of eggs, given the size of our large family. Sometimes a hen would build a nest some distance from the hen house, and when found, we would fill a pail with water and place the eggs in the water. If they stayed at the bottom of the pail, they were pronounced fresh. We would try and prevent any of the birds from flying too far away by clipping some of their wing feathers. I loved to be the first on the scene when chicks were hatched, and once they dried, they looked very cute.

We also had chores to do before going to school in the morning, when we would give my parents a hand with milking the two cows, either inside the byre or out on the croft in better weather. If a cow was in the habit of kicking while being milked, we would tie a fetter on both its hind legs. The cows spent most of their time outdoors in the better weather, and would get annoyed by the clegs while being milked. The fields were lovely and smelt nice with flowers like spotted daisy, milkwort, honeysuckle, primrose, spotted dorkies and bluebells abundant. I firmly believe that as soon as artificial fertilizers became widely used, it did irreversible damage to our wild flowers and fauna.

From the age of about seven, we were expected to take a turn at being first up in the morning to help put the house in order. This would mean taking the ashes out from the old stove, taking peats in from the stack and building a fire, taking two buckets to fetch water from the well, which was about a quarter of a mile away and then sweeping the floor. After that, the rest of the siblings were allowed up, but you were in charge.

Incidentally, I still love the smell of burning peat, but the process of cutting and stacking it could, at times, be murder. One time at the peat cutting, the midgies were so bad that I ran home and covered my face in syrup, so that they would stick in it rather than bite me. You certainly had to be adaptable and react to circumstances as they arose.

Our water was drawn from a well, which was communal, and there were several on Grimsay. People took care of them and took their turn to clean them and so forth. If it was a natural spring then it didn't need much cleaning and the water was always lovely. We called this a fuaran. I've never tasted water like that, and it's such a shame that with all these chemicals and radioactive fallout, you're scared to drink anything now.

We were taught to use a gun from a very early age (probably under age). I didn't really have the patience for it, but my brother Angus was a good shot. I wasn't bad at catching snipe though, and cormorant was a bit of a speciality of mine.

These all provided good eating, although we were pretty rough and ready about how they were prepared. I remember once being out on the Monach Isles with a chap from South Uist called Willie Holister. We shot a cormorant, and had eaten it within an hour. We shot it, tied a string around it, slit the skin off in a oner (which is easier when the bird is warm) and chucked it in a pan of boiling water.

In wintertime we milked the cows in the byre, and fed any calves that we had. The family cats would get a saucer of this milk, but not too much or they wouldn't keep down the vermin like rats and mice. The fodder, either corn or hay, was kept in the barn and fed to the cows morning and night. We sometimes thrashed oats 'corca mòr' and 'corca beag' with a special wooden switch or flail, and kept the seed to be sown the following spring. The byre had to be cleaned each day and the muck barrowed out and formed into a 'tor'. Sometimes we constructed a 'flagish' or compost heap, which consisted of sand, straw, muck and seaweed. The winter gales washed up a lot of seaweed, which we forked ashore and made use of. It was all very good for the black soil on our croft.

We also had a good vegetable garden fenced nearby, and father bought some nice fir trees from Lochaline which he planted here to look nice and keep shelter for the various plants growing there. When going to school one day, I remember one of my sisters getting hold of an axe, and carrying out some chopping on the afore mentioned trees, for which I got a real leathering.

From a very young age, we were taught to care for this vegetable patch, each child having his or her own allotted area to tend. There were probably two very good reasons for this regimentation, namely competition and accountability. We grew cabbage, kale, lettuce, carrots, peas, leeks, beetroot, turnips and parsnips. We all became good at this important task.

We would collect the necessary fertilizer, which could consist of seaweed, sand or cow and hen manure, and trench the ground uniformly to a depth of some six to nine inches. After that, we carefully applied the manure; not too little, not too much. This was then covered over with soil from the next digging, making sure the patch was well drained, and in our case the main drain ran into the sea. At planting time the seeds were sown as carefully as possible. We used to take pride in these tasks, and I'm sure it helped us grow to being disciplined.

This small garden also had room for four corn or haystacks. The base of the stack used to be constructed with old timbers, stones and, sometimes, scrap iron. My father often put some of the hay crop at the bottom of the rick to help prevent rats and mice getting at the corn.

Building the corn or haystack properly was an art in itself, with the end result having to be safe from winter gales and uniform in line and shape. It was a two-man job, with one on the stack and one forking up to him. A spade was also used to tuck in protruding corn and to keep the shape correct. The last, but most important, job was to rope the stack down with ciadh (heather rope), as sisal rope was expensive. Then there were up to a dozen specially selected stones which we used to weigh it all down. Sometimes we found bits of netting on the shore that proved very useful for securing the stack.

My late father took great pride in his croft, making sure it was properly drained and fenced, a job that he began over fifty years ago. I clearly remember, as a very young boy,

24

helping him with this, by handing him staples as he secured the fence. Most, if not all, of the posts he collected came from the shores of Heisker, as a great deal of timber came ashore during the second war, along with other useful flotsam and jetsam. Unfortunately, most of this came from ships sunk during hostilities. Once, my cousin, Willie Stewart, even came across a cask of alcohol on the shore, and a very good time was had by all.

We had open and closed drains on our croft, with the closed variety being a work of art. A person cut a sod of earth from specially selected ground in the shape of a triangle, with a slice cut out at the sharp end so that water could flow. The process of drainage was very skilled, and we sometimes had to construct a culvert over drains so that people and cattle could cross carefully. We used stone for this construction, although some people used hard, dry peat.

As you know, we kept a horse, which was very useful for work on the croft, but my father liked to keep up to date with modern developments, and we were the first family on the island to have a tractor, albeit a motor plough which you walked behind. It had a pulley, and you could also saw wood and things like that with it as well.

I remember very well the day him and I went to Carinish to collect it. It was a Japanese machine called an 'Anzani' with rubber wheels and a pair of iron wheels also. My father constructed a trailer from an old lorry chassis and it had its own wooden box. It proved to be a great help for the ploughing, and also for carrying materials such as peat, manure, stones and fencing and it went at a very fast walking pace in top gear. Dad was very proud of the tractor, and there are bits of it to be seen on the croft to this day. In addition, it found dad a lot of extra work ploughing for other people, sometimes going as far as Claddach Carinish.

I accompanied him once to the home of an old merchant seaman who had asked him to plough his croft for him. The old man, 'Domhnull Ruadh Eilean', had a lovely gold pocket watch, which very much intrigued me, and he had a pet monkey, which kept me spellbound. Domhnull had spent most of his time at sea with the 'Brocklebank' shipping company and had bought the monkey in India or somewhere on his travels.

Actually, it's funny, but there was another family at that time, by the name of Newlands. They were travelling people that came to Uist every year and they owned a pet monkey called 'Chicago'. Betty Newlands would show us youngsters the cute, wee animal provided that we gave her sixpence. She had him hidden in her pinafore, and he immediately appeared as soon as the transaction was completed. Poor 'Chicago' met a tragic end though. Betty died of cancer, and her husband thought that the monkey had caused this, so he drowned him. I can mind seeing the wee thing strung up with a stone tied to it at Gramasdale pier. I felt so sad for it.

Dogs were also an integral part of our life, and we had many of them on the croft when I was growing up. One of the first that I remember was a dog called 'Floss'. The poor animal contracted distemper, and one sad morning she came to my parents' bed, begging to be let outside. A day or so later, we found her drowned at Linne na Dairbe. She had decided to end her life that way. We also had a lovely dog, coloured white with a few brown spots, called 'Shirley', after the actress Shirley Temple. She was a very good sheep dog, being strong and obedient, and able to handle the strong wedders that my father had bought from Uncle Alec.

My parents had another wonderful dog who was capable of going to the local Post Office and bringing back letters and small parcels. This animal also had a sad end, being caught in the revolving shaft of my father's boat. His tail was badly damaged and he had to be put down. Another dog called 'Winnie' would gather the sheep and make sure that they would follow her to where my father wanted them to go. This

26

meant dog, sheep, Dad, in that order rather than the other way around.

We had other pets as well. My sister Morag had a tortoise, which went missing for weeks, being found eventually outside John MacLean's shop. When I went to the agricultural college in Aberdeen, I brought home two guinea pigs, one each for my sisters Effie and Margaret. I would tease the girls by saying, "Hold them by their tail and they'll complain." Of course, just like a Manx cat, guinea pigs don't have tails.

The 'lambing' was a very busy time on the croft, and you had to be up early in the morning, in case the crows got to the lambs while they were being born. Some of the ewes had twins, and, on more than one occasion, gave birth to triplets. My mother was very fond of sheep, and I have a photograph taken of her when she would have been about sixteen holding a pet lamb.

My father was very good with sheep, and enjoyed working with them on the croft. People used to laugh, but he was so often among them that they knew his voice. The sheep would follow him everywhere, meaning that he often had no need of a sheepdog, which in itself was quite unique.

Cameras were rare in those days, although my mother had a nice box camera which she used for family snaps. A friend of our family, Mrs. Ross, from Nairn, took a family photograph of all nine of us standing on a small hill at the back of our home. Archie, the youngest of the family, had not been born yet. This would have been in the early 50s. Years later, while I was a radio officer on a trip to Bombay, I had the snap enlarged and coloured. I gave an approximate idea of the colour of our clothes to the Indian gentleman who did this for me, and it hangs proudly on my bedroom wall to this day. In the photograph, my father is wearing his yachting uniform, and he looks very smart.

He wore it on the day that he was presented to Her Majesty the Queen, on the pier at Lochmaddy. The Duke of Edinburgh asked him, "Where did you get those brass buttons?" to which my father replied, "I earned them Your Highness!"

Back in my father's younger days there weren't so many yachts about, it still being very much the preserve of the rich and privileged. People like my father got seasonal jobs skippering these vessels, which earned you five pounds wages and a uniform. Dad sailed yachts for people like Lord Mosely, whose boat was based in the Menai Straits, in Wales. He also skippered for Dorothea Howard of Rhu, Dumbarton. Some of the owners raced on the Clyde in clubs such as the Royal Corinthian Clyde Yacht Club, in which the Duke of Edinburgh himself used to compete.

As I said earlier, Grimsay was a tidal island up until the early 1960s, when the causeway was opened. Our means of transport to what we called the mainland, Benbecula or North Uist, consisted of boats, getting a lift in a cart or gig, if the tide allowed, or Shanks' Pony. This was no bad thing. Using boats and horses and carts, you got very used to the way nature worked. You didn't need tide tables, it was all in your head.

I can remember going to dances in Benbecula, and having to swim the ford to do so. I would take off my clothes and tie them with my braces in a package above my head to keep them dry, and then make my crossing. What a carry on to get to a dance, but I suppose there were only two or three dances in a year at that time. Nowadays there are two or three a day!

Fishing was probably the most important industry on the island, along with crofting, and it definitely took precedence during the summer. There were two main harbours on the island. The people in Ceallan would tell you that theirs is the most important, but Ardnastruban was equally important.

My father and John Archie MacVicar, and sometimes John Archie's brother Donald, used to fish with the fishing

28

boat we had at the time called 'Effie-Ann'. The boat was originally built on the Monach Isles, by a boat builder, name of Murray, from Ness in Lewis, who was known better as 'an t-saor beag', the wee carpenter. As part of their fishing, they used to kill a few big grey seals every season. These would be taken home and cut up for various different uses. The wee sections of blubber, or 'Craiseag', as we called it, would be cut, and the oil taken, which would be fed to the cattle. It was almost like a form of medicine. It put a sheen on their skin and cleaned them out.

The sea played a huge part in everyone's lives on Grimsay. We were surrounded by it, and our lives were lived according to its rhythms and its cycles. We depended on it for our sustenance and our livelihoods.

When I look at our old home at the moment, the front is almost into the sea, and a lot of the stuff we took home, like groceries, would come in from the sea, to the front of the house. Now, since the road was built, everything comes to the back door in a car. There were four or five small grocers shops when I was young. If you wanted bread or something, it could be nearly a week on the 'Dunara Castle' coming from Glasgow. If you had bread that didn't have grey mould on it, you were doing well. For this reason, much of our baking was done at home. Our mothers would provide all kinds of bread, scones and other treats for us, and some of the fathers were good at baking too.

My father was a 'Jack of all trades', and if he were alive he wouldn't allow me to say 'master of none'. He was first and foremost a crofter and fisherman, but he dabbled in many other sidelines also. He was the kind of unofficial auctioneer on Grimsay. For example, if someone was flitting, my father may have been asked to sell their Rayburn for them, or maybe other articles of furniture that they didn't need. He also doubled as a

The Nicholson brothers; left to right: Angus, John, Ewen and Archie

butcher sometimes as well. My father's brother had the farm of Heaval, and father would buy wedders off him and slaughter them and sell the meat on. He would often slaughter three sheep a week. I used to hate it as it seemed very cruel, all the sheep being killed with a knife. Nowadays you have to use a humane killer. All the family would then be employed going around with parcels of mutton for people. He certainly wasn't trained as a butcher, but necessity being the mother of invention, he was able to turn his hand to it. There was a man near us, Archie MacVicar, who used to help my father, and my mother was very good at using the offal and leftovers for puddings. He also used to buy wool off people, and he would go to Loch Carnan and buy big barrels of salt mackerel, which were probably sold to the same people who bought the wool or the mutton, so he was an enterprising kind of guy.

He had been at sea himself, and, as you know, skippered yachts at one time. He had also been deep sea, and had seen a bit of life and a bit of the world I suppose. He always tried to better himself, and liked to be at the forefront of any new development or innovation.

Radios were few and far between, but my father had one of the first sets on the island, with the dry battery and the accumulator. You had to go to someone with a generator, and there were two or three people who had these on the island. It meant that they could have electric light, and they could charge your accumulator. Of course, if you didn't have a generator you still had your Tilly lamp and your lantern for going out to attend to cattle, and for milking them in the byre.

It wasn't uncommon for us to go next door to our neighbours if our own radio wasn't working, especially if there was a boxing match on. Some of us youngsters loved listening to the boxing. It would be a big outing if the likes of Joe Louis or Rocky Marciano were fighting. My father always talked about boxers he had met in Glasgow, like Benny Lynch. In fact, I myself was fortunate enough to meet Benny Lynch's

31

widow. Poor Benny turned to alcohol, and didn't have to seek the many scroungers who tend to accompany such a tragic figure.

My father could remember being in a bar once with Benny Lynch, when a big Lewisman decided to show off by picking Benny up and plonking him on the bar counter. Mockingly the Lewisman looked Benny Lynch up and down and said, "Yer no much now." Lynch never hesitated and laid the Lewisman out with one punch. Right out of the game! He was finished as a boxer by then, but obviously hadn't lost his touch.

Dad actually boxed a bit himself. I don't know if he was boasting, but there was once quite a famous French boxer by the name of Georges Carpentier who my father had a bit of a run in with. While at sea, my father and a friend of his from South Uist were sometimes in the habit of going ashore and drinking their money. Later, and penniless, they would have a pretend 'scrap' in the street, and if this attracted a crowd, they would put a hat around to raise some capital. Anyway, they ended up ashore somewhere in France one night and their antics attracted the attention of this famous French boxer, who challenged my father to a fight. Dad accepted and managed to catch Carpentier straight off with a quick one. However, with the very next punch, Carpentier managed to flatten my father, and that was the end of the fight.

He was also, as I said earlier, a county councillor. He always had a keen interest in politics, and seemed to like 'spouting' on the subject. He was a real Labour man, although he always talked about the 'Welsh Wizard', Lloyd George. He started off in local council in Lochmaddy, and eventually got to the county council in Inverness. Of course, in those days, you had to pay your own fare, which meant us missing out on money that we should really have been having as a family, and my mother had quite a struggle bringing us up. But his duty as a councillor was important to my father and he was a man of strong principles. He taught us all the value of really hard work.

He used to help people to read and write letters too, maybe if their schooling hadn't been quite what it should. He was a community minded man, and highly educated, although basically self taught. He was the youngest of his family, and I think that if he had received a proper education, he would have gone a long way. He would try anything to turn a coin.

He was very much a family man, who was proud of his children, and expected us to set a good example at all times. This was never better illustrated than on a Sunday, when we were mobilised for our morning worship.

My father would shout "church parade." He would line us up, and make sure that the height of our socks were the same so that no one could say that Andrew Nicholson's children weren't turned out immaculately. My mother, on the other hand, had a slightly ambivalent attitude towards her fellow church-goers. She used to say, "They'll not speak to you on Sunday, and they'll rob you on Monday."

I remember him once shooting a grey mullet from the doorstep of the house. He could see the fin bobbing up and down in the water and managed to shoot it in the head. He was a great man for the gun.

When I was at home the other day, a cousin of mine showed me some letters that had been written to and from my uncle Ewen while he was away fighting in the Great War. It was particularly moving. My uncle Ewen was a very good shot, and taught my father how to shoulder a gun.

An aunty of mine used to steal cartridges from the shop on Grimsay to give to my father. This was to help him keep down the rabbit population, although my aunty soon got fed up with all the rabbits that were being taken home. One day, my father turned up at the house with four small rabbits, and my aunty told my uncle Ewen in her letter that they were only the size of a decent rat.

My uncle Ewen replied by sending home three feathers taken from a heron he had shot somewhere in Flanders. I saw these feathers for the first time last Sunday. They had been kept so well by his mother. It is strange, but there is an old Highland belief that it is bad luck to kill a heron, and I hope this had no part in my uncle's death in 1916.

He had emigrated to Canada about 1910, and found work with the logging somewhere in Saskatchewan. There was no shortage of work, and many of these Highland emigrants did very well. I had a cousin, MacDeirmid, who became mayor of Deel in Florida, which was a smaller place then than it is now, but still quite an honour.

Ewen was conscripted into one of the Canadian 'Highland' regiments, and was killed in France, at the age of twenty-four, in 1916. My father, who was fourteen at the time, must have been pretty psychic, because he came down the stairs in the post office with tears in his eyes. When my grandparents asked him what was wrong, he told them that something had happened to his brother Ewen, and, sure enough, Ewen was shot at around the same time. It is terrible to think that had things not turned out as bad as they did in the first war, my uncle would have been safe enough in Canada.

My mother was a real hard worker as well. She used to have to do the family's washing in a loch. You had to build a big fire and then avail yourself of a big cauldron, in which you would boil water and eventually wash your clothes. This had to be done at least once a week.

She was also involved in the production of tweed. I can remember, as a child, being sent to scrape lichen and what we called 'crotal' off the rocks to use in the production. It gave a lovely colour to the material, when you boiled it in a tub. Sometimes the women or children would jump into the tub to stamp on the material as it was mixing with the dye. I was told this story in Vancouver once, that long before I was born, my granny jumped into a tub to do this very job, only to find that someone had thrown a broken bottle in too, and doctors and nurses weren't exactly plentiful at that time.

The waulking tradition had pretty much died out by the time I came along. However, I do remember witnessing a waulking on a couple of occasions, as a small child. I can vaguely remember half a dozen women sitting round big sheets of corrugated zinc working at the tweed.

Virtually everything that we take for granted today had to be made or home spun. Everything had at least three or four jobs associated with it, so you had to be willing to graft. It made you a very resourceful person though, and people were happy with their lot. My uncle Angus lived in the really old style in a house that was badly in need of a few mod cons and comforts that the government would have provided, but Angus wouldn't hear of it. He was quite happy with his pipe and his dog, and what more did he need?

In all honesty, we knew very little about the outside world, apart from maybe the stories brought home from merchant seaman returning from a long voyage. As a small child, I can remember, vaguely, planes landing on Benbecula during the war; 'Flying Fortresses' and suchlike. That was really as far as the war touched us. Obviously, our young men were overseas fighting just like everyone else, my own father was on the convoys, and we certainly worried about them, but there wasn't the same evidence of war as elsewhere. Rationing didn't really affect us all that much, as nature, as usual, had provided for us. Looking back, it must have been a worrying time for my mother. What would she have done if my father had not returned and she had been left with a young family? I suppose we would have managed, the community would have rallied round, as they did for countless others.

I have a feeling that people were kinder when I was a child. Maybe they had to be. After all, in a tightly knit community like ours, where you relied on other people everyday, it didn't do to be constantly falling out with your neighbours, you never knew when you might need them, so people tended to get on and help each other. It was great visiting people. You didn't need an invitation. You just went. They were either in or out. I liked visiting older people, and felt that I was always learning something about my heritage, which they had heard from people long ago, and were only to happy to pass on. There were many wonderful storytellers on the island, especially some of the old men who had been deep sea and travelled round the world. It seemed to me that most of the houses were what we called a 'Taigh Ceilidh', a ceilidh house.

As a child, one of my favourite pastimes was making model boats. These would be fashioned from wood, or whatever was to hand, and finished with a sail. After that I graduated to building my own raft, and oh, that was real deep sea stuff. You got a hold of a couple of old sacks, which were joined together to form a sail. You added to this a big long pole, which would be used to push you along in the bay in front of the house. Just ideal for the job. My father also taught us all how to swim. He was a very good swimmer, and the way he taught us was to make us paddle out so far on his back and then swim for the shore. It was a handy thing being able to swim, and was maybe somewhat unusual, as many of the boys I knew who were at sea couldn't swim at all.

I suppose life was fairly ordered, and it had to be, to survive on a small island like Grimsay. Our community was built on a code of respect; respect for your family, respect for your neighbours and respect for your elders.

Each communal event, be it work or recreation was planned carefully, and everyone, from youngest to oldest, played their part, with weddings being a particular favourite of mine. It was great going to a wedding even if just for the feed you would get. A wedding was a big occasion, and the whole community would have been there. It was still very much an old fashioned affair.

As often as not, weddings celebrations would be held in a barn, or the schoolhouse if they could get it. The women had to do a lot of the work, preparing hens and mutton and other things to eat and drink. Nothing would have happened without them.

Wedding dances were wonderful too. We were lucky on Grimsay, as there were usually good musicians locally who could be hired for the night. There were quite a few melodeon players and pipers. I loved going to dances in my younger days. The master of ceremonies, or 'Fear an Taigh' as we called him, would always be some local worthy. He'd have a jar of whisky inside him, and he'd have you taking your partners for the same old dances all night; military two-step etc.

Sometimes you would have a lone piper for the whole night, and sometimes just one guy with a melodeon, it all depended. You were doing well if you had two.

Dances tended to last for a minimum of four hours, say ten till two, although most went on much longer. They were unlicensed affairs, so you had to take refreshments with you, which would be secreted outside the hall, 'Dutch courage' as we used to call it.

Dances on Grimsay were held in the schoolhouse, but, as I got older, I loved going to the dances in the gym in Balivanich, which became a very famous venue indeed. I can still see Iain MacLachlan, his eyes closed with drink, playing his melodeon. He must have been almost mechanical, on autopilot. I can recall his step-father playing with him as well.

I suppose things have changed, and maybe for the better. It was often the way that parents would decide what you were going to do with your life, which wasn't always a good thing. Things are different now, and I believe that you should be allowed to decide (within reason) what you are going to do. Funnily enough, I didn't have a hankering for the sea at first. I wanted to become a joiner, but my father said, "You couldn't even make a spurtle for porridge," so that was the end of that.

An early family photograph before my brother Archie was born. L to R Father, Ann, John, Mother, Margaret, Angus, Morag, Effie and myself.

Today North Uist, Tomorrow the World

From August 1949 until June 1950, I attended Bayhead Junior Secondary School, in North Uist. The head teacher there was Mr Donald John Boyd. He was a master of seven languages.

I believe his first school was actually Mallaig during the 1930s. I know this because he was very fond of one of his pupils in Mallaig, Andrew Johnstone, whom I knew myself. Andrew would sometimes come and live at Temple View, Carinish, with James MacLean and his wife, and Mr Boyd always left strict instructions that they were to 'only speak Gaelic to that boy', who would have been about twelve or thirteen at the time.

I thought that Bayhead School was very big in comparison to Grimsay school, which it was, although I enjoyed the experience fine, as my dad got me digs with the MacDonald family (Erchie Eoghan), at Ardban, Kyles. The parents were called Archie (Erchie Eoghan) and Morag, and they had five children; Flora, Ewen, Jessie, Agnes and Ena, who is still in the family home. I was very happy with this hard working and lovely family.

The lodgings were only a pound a week, and we got really great food and dairy produce. It was wonderful, and I was only too glad to help with the work on their big croft, especially with the corn. I also helped at the peat cutting and with milking cows. They had a proper tractor and trailer, which was quite a status symbol in those days. We would load the trailer with seaweed, and 'tangle' when it was blown up from an Atlantic storm, which always helped to make their potato crop a big and bounteous one.

We did a wee bit of sea trout fishing as well, one for the pot, although there happened to be quite a lot of pots about! We netted these, which led to Archie getting into a bit of trouble with one of the local gamekeepers. The keeper in question came to remonstrate with Archie about his actions, but was sent packing, with Archie telling him, "Away and ask your father why you've got such rosy cheeks, all that salmon that you ate when you were young, and behave yourself!"

Another time, a water bailiff arrived at Archie's. It was a driech, horrible day. The bailiff asked him where would be the best place to catch a sea trout or salmon with his rod. Archie knew exactly what was on the man's mind, and put him in a place where he was unlikely to catch anything if he was there yet.

He knew fine well that if he had shown the man a place where fish were plentiful, then the game would have been up.

Mrs MacDonald came from Mull, and she was a lovely woman. Their children were Ewen, who had left school when I arrived, Flora, who had also left school, Jessie, Agnes and Ena, who was ages with me, and I'm delighted to say that Ena was presented this year (2006) with the MBE for services to agriculture. Her sister Jessie was laughing, she said it stood for 'milk, butter and eggs.' Ena has done an awful lot for crofting and she certainly deserved that honour.

Myself and Ewen MacDonald were very keen on visiting the old bodachs and cailleachs in the area and having a ceilidh with them. I don't suppose we were the most well behaved boys either, cracking jokes at the expense of these poor people. We went to this poor woman's house, who was very, very kind, although maybe a wee bit clarty. She gave us tea and dumpling, which had wee bits of hair on it. So I decided to stick mine underneath the bench that I was sitting on. Unfortunately her dog decided to retrieve it from there and leave it on the sand covered floor, in full view of the woman of the house. We were then immediately escorted out of the door. She didn't take it well at all. I should have put it in my pocket, instead of embarrassing the poor woman, but I wasn't going to eat hair was I?

Ewen MacDonald and I were forever getting into mischief of one sort or another. Never anything terribly bad you understand, but enough to keep our parents on their toes.

I knew that my parents had been invited to a wedding in Loch Eyport, and myself and Ewen decided that we would go too. We only had the one bicycle, so we took turn about of peddling or going on the cross bar for a distance of about eight miles, which didn't bother us as we were young and fit. We were quite hardy.

We turned up at the thatched cottage where the wedding was being held, only to get merry hell from my father. "But our family was invited," I told him.

"Aye, but not you specifically," he said.

I enjoyed Bayhead School, although it was markedly different to what I had been used to. It was a bigger school for a start, and there was also a wider curriculum. The two main subjects that we had in Bayhead that I didn't have in Grimsay Public School were science and woodwork. We had singing as well, but unfortunately I couldn't put two notes together, and still can't. There was a tuning fork on the go, and we would clown around, although you couldn't do that if Mr Boyd was present. He had a terrible temper on him. I think he actually took a bit of a drink, and he probably had a hangover as often as not.

He didn't mind you operating at say 50% if you weren't academically inclined, but he hated the idea of you being lazy or underachieving if he thought you could do better. There was one girl from Grimsay who got 98% in some test or other, and received the most terrible belting because she hadn't got 100%. Anyway, her father ended up going to see Mr Boyd, and gave him a thrashing! That was the way things were settled.

I suppose, myself, I was one of those 50% guys, but Mr Boyd seemed to be quite fond of me, because at least he knew

I was trying. It was just that he couldn't have got an awful lot more out of me.

He was actually a Latin teacher as far as I know, and he taught Gaelic also, and another couple of things. I seem to remember that we got an awful lot of homework, which you just had to do. There was no messing about. Mind you, we did a bit of copying off one another as well. Sometimes I would get Archie MacDonald's children to help me with things that I couldn't do myself.

I liked Bayhead an awful lot. It was another wonderful community, much as I had been used to at home, and I took an immediate interest in the people and the history of the locality.

There is a big rock, or wee hill, in Bayhead, called Creag a h'Astein, near Balamor. They used to hold open air communion services there nearly one hundred years ago. Possibly two or three denominations used that hill because there were so many people going to the communions that their churches weren't big enough. Can you imagine that today?

Religion was still a very important part of community life during my stay there. At school I knew the MacAulays of Kirkibost quite well. That was the same family as the publicans in Creaggory. Old MacAulay was very good with sheep and cattle. He didn't have much education, he could hardly write his name, but, my goodness, he knew the hoof of an animal. They were Free Church, and would call on Archie Eoghan at communion times. Mrs MacDonald would provide a big meal for them, and, although our food was excellent, we got a wee bit more on communion days.

I suppose I considered myself a bit of a city slicker, and was often to be found indulging in a spot of retail therapy in 'downtown' Bayhead. I liked going to Floraidh Thormaid's shop. She was a character, and we used to get a laugh at her. She was nice. Her shop was in Bailemor. In those days I believed in Christmas, so it was a great thing if I took wee presents home for my brothers and sisters. And sweets that you got in North Uist were much better than sweets tha would get in Grimsay. And the sweets that you got in Glasₓ were fantastic. The same kind of sweets, but where they can. from mattered. Being the oldest of eight, I had to get seven wee parcels ready. I didn't have much money, but I did the best I could with what I had.

I left Bayhead School in June 1950. I would have been about fourteen or fifteen. I suppose my poor dad was trying to knock some of the nonsense out of my head. Even then, it was full of nonsense; chasing girls and all that, and I still hadn't really thought about going to sea. In fact, I didn't know what I was going to do.

My dad wanted me to go to Balmacara, near Kyle of Lochalsh, which was a very interesting school. I don't know what you would call it now, but they taught a lot of practical subjects like technical drawing, woodwork, gardening, crop husbandry and so on. You also had to work pretty hard on the farm as well, and I spent two very enjoyable years there.

I thought the school was a huge place, being used to the wee places in Uist. Meeting all the other boys there was good. It was something I enjoyed. I don't suppose I had been on the mainland before, so I suppose it was something of a culture shock.

My cousin Archie MacLean was also at the school, which helped, although we weren't always a good influence on each other. We were sailing back from Uist to Kyle once, on a boat that went via Mallaig when, by hook or by crook, we managed to get a hold of a bottle of beer. Needless to say, we got a wee bit out of order. Archie decided to give this poor hiker jip that was travelling in steerage with us. The hiker said he would report us to the skipper, and Archie told him, "If you don't shut up, I'll go through you like a dose of salts." The guy reported us to the chief officer, who came down and gave us merry hell, and so he should have done. This was the first but by no means the last time that I would find myself in trouble with my superiors on board a ship! And that wasn't our only mishap.

In those days your mother always made sure you had plenty of sandwiches and dumplings for any journey that you might have to make, and we were heavily laden when we came ashore in Mallaig. We decided to visit a wee tearoom down on the pier, where we ordered a pot of tea, and then produced our own sandwiches, which prompted one hell of a telling off from the woman in charge. I don't know if she threw us out, but we left anyway. It wasn't the done thing to take your own food. How green can you get?

Another friend of mine was Alec Angus MacDonald, who also ended up as a radio officer deep sea like myself. He was quite civilised compared to me though, and eventually became a house captain at school.

I don't suppose that many of the boys from Balmacara ended up going to sea, as the purpose of the school was really to train you for more land based jobs in agriculture and the like. None of us were really academically gifted, and again, the purpose of the school was to educate you in more practical subjects. I suppose it meant that you got, at best, an average education, but I like to think that I educated myself as I went through the world.

We got up to all the usual schoolboy pranks in the dormitories. Quite often boys would receive a parcel of food from home, which was best to be left unopened until under the cover of darkness. Of course, the other boys would be listening out for the rustle of paper, and when spotted, the lights would go on and the owner of the parcel would be 'encouraged' to share out the contents with everyone else.

I had a sideline in picking winkles, which would be sent by train, after possibly conning someone into taking them to Kyle, direct to Billingsgate Market, in London. This wasn't always a money-spinner though, because you were often at the mercy of unscrupulous salesmen, who would just say that the winkles weren't in any fit state to sell when they reached London.

Balmacara had been a private house at one time, and was let to the education authorities in the same way as the other school in the locality, Duncraig, which was exclusively for girls. I believe the navy took it over after it finished its life as a school.

A Balmacara School photo. I'm standing second from the left in the third row.

At that time there was a teacher in Duncraig, Kay Matheson, who was one of those responsible for the taking of the 'Stone of Destiny.' I also remember that the matron in the girls' hostel was known as 'the Crow.' Funnily enough, I was visiting some friends on the east coast last year, and happened to be on a bus going to Aberdeen, when I got talking to a woman who had attended Duncraig School. When I asked her when she had attended the school, she said to me, "Oh, it was a while after you Ewen, but you'll remember the Crow."

Our Matron, Miss MacLennan, was a different kettle of fish. She was very kind, and would even darn our socks for us,

45

as she knew that most of us didn't have much money. One of my teachers, Kenny Gollan, became famous for sailing wee boats around Plockton. There was also the caretaker who stayed in the gate-house of Balmacara School. He was a Harrisman, and one of his jobs was to look after a wee boat that the boys got the use of. Anyway, I decided to steal the boat one night and sail it to Kyle. Of course, I did a wee bit of fishing on the way too. All my childhood training on Grimsay came into its own. I stayed well into the shore and kept out of the current. I felt very important going on such a big voyage, and returned the boat safely, but that didn't stop me catching it from the caretaker, Finlay MacLennan, when I got back.

The two principal teachers were quite strict, Mr Marwick and Mr Sutherland. We were made to go to church, whichever church you belonged to, and were taught very strong morals.

If only I had paid more heed to this. One year I decided to stay on at Balmacara to help with the harvest, and didn't the bold Ewen decided to go to a dance in Dornie. That would have been fine, but I managed to get a hold of a half bottle of whisky and got well sozzled. The next day, I wasn't able to do my work because of the hangover, and the principal was near jumping off the floor with rage, and he reported me to my father, who gave me a hell of a thrashing when I eventually went home. That was my first main encounter with 'King Alcohol.'

I was actually caught once more, this time with a quarter bottle, at Balmacara. The offending article was found under my pillow, and, once more, the headmaster was jumping his height. He said, "Right Nicholson, explain this."

'Well sir," says I, "Santa Claus always gives you a present depending on what you would prefer, and in my case he thought I would like a quarter bottle of whisky."

We had a lot of laughs. Sometimes we would go to parties in Duncraig. We had a fancy dress party once where I dressed up like a hen, squawking along as I went. I don't remember whether I frightened the Crow or not.

I still keep in touch with some of the other boys. A couple of months ago, there was a knock at the door. Here was Kenny 'Jeck' MacKenzie, from Lochcarron. A great shinty player in his day, though now he's old like me. He had loads to tell me and I had loads to tell him, although I asked him if he would mind coming back in the winter when I'm not so busy.

I don't suppose there was much planning on my part for what I would do on leaving Balmacara. It was certainly more the case in those days that your parents mapped out your life for you, which wasn't always a good idea.

My dad, as I said a while ago, put a stop to any notion of me becoming a joiner. He knew a man in Benbecula, Mr Kerr, who worked for the Department of Agriculture, and dad had designs that I should be like him. He wanted me to go in for agriculture, and so, after finishing in Balmacara he sent me to Craibstone Agricultural School in Aberdeen, which did a year long certificate in agriculture.

There were probably between fifteen and twenty of us in the class, many of whom were older than me. Being mostly of farming stock, some of these boys had access to money, and they used to take me to the posh hotels in Aberdeen. We'd be draming away there like it was going out of fashion, which I thought was very manly at the time.

I liked going to the city of Aberdeen, and I used to enjoy watching the men playing the outdoor drafts with the huge long poles. It was an amazing experience for someone who had considered Kyle of Lochalsh a metropolis.

We had excellent teachers there, and were taught animal husbandry, crop husbandry, cattle rearing and how to keep pigs. I suppose I was ahead of the game as far as the practical side was concerned, although I struggled with the academic content because I didn't have a particularly good education. We were also taught a bit of the blacksmith's trade, and I've still got a cold chisel that I made in Craibstone. I have it on the boat yet.

You were also given a certain number of cows that you had to look after and milk yourself, which was quite a responsibility, and one I took very seriously.

My fellow students were from 'a the airts', as they say. There was one lad, Robin Warrington, from the Channel Islands, and another from Ireland, one from Redcar in Yorkshire, and a Dunnet Halcro from Orkney, who came from a family of chicken farmers.

We were regular attendants at dances in Kintore and the Railway Hall in Inverurie, usually chasing women. We also started drinking in a place that's still going, the Four Mile Inn, which was something of a landmark in Kintore. We'd be walking down there, and we'd pass the Rowett Research Institute, which was at the cutting edge of science, even in those days.

I went to Findourie Farm in Brechin, on the completion of my certificate at Craibstone College. I can't honestly remember why I ended up at Findourie. I must have made enquiries, or maybe one of my friends at the school would have had a contact there. There were, after all, a few boys at Craibstone from the Angus area. There was a guy Robertson, from near Forfar, a farm called 'Heatherstacks.' They're still farming there yet, and I know this because of a woman I took out on my boat only last year. She knew of the farm, and was pretty sure that the Robertsons still have it. I don't suppose it's the variety I knew who'll be farming it now, but you never know. Anyway, it may have been him that suggested Findourie to me.

Findourie was a dairy farm owned by J.R Barron, and was very modern, even fifty years ago. There were one hundred and forty five milking cows, mostly Ayrshires, but we had milking parlours kitted out with all the latest technology, which made our work much easier.

48

The bad news was that you had to get up at half past two every morning, but you soon got used to it, although it was quite hard going if you'd been to a dance until half past one. You were allowed back to your bed at half past six, if you wanted, once you got the cows milked and back into the field again.

I stayed in a bothy with three or four other boys. The bothy consisted of one main room with a big open fire, and a couple of small bedrooms. We did all our own cooking and cleaning, so you quickly became quite adept domestically. You got free milk, free potatoes and free coal, but everything else you had to buy or organise yourself, so you became quite good at household economics too. When you're young nothing bothers you, and we had everything we needed, so we were perfectly happy. I suppose the bothy way of life was really coming to an end then, so I'm glad that I got a chance to experience what it was like to be an 'orra loon.'

There would have probably been the best part of twenty men working on that farm, which is staggering by today's standards. There would have been head cattle men, dairymen, a grieve, you name it. It was big time farming, and J.R Barron owned another two farms, one near Dundee and one near Perth, which I believe the family are still running.

They had every implement you could think of. Grass driers, for drying out the hay, which created the most beautiful smell off the bales. It was so beautiful and green; real clover. It was full of goodness. Their farms were run exceptionally well. The welfare of the animals was paramount, and you were expected to be exceptionally clean at all times. The animals were exceptional beasts, and Mr Barron won a lot of prizes displaying them at agricultural shows.

They used to take the cattle to Ayr and places like that. It was quite a performance trimming and cleaning the cattle beforehand, but worth it if they won. It was usually just the head dairymen who would have gone, although I was lucky and got to go once. It was quite a journey in a cattle float. Off we went to Perth, and then via Glasgow to Ayr. A great day out.

They grew a lot of strawberries as well, which was, and still is, very common in that area. It used to be a treat to be in under the nets scoffing strawberries at six in the morning. In fact, they grew all kinds of fruit. A friend of mine and I decided to go nicking apples one night. Findourie farm had a wonderful orchard and their apples were highly prized, which made our operation all the more exciting. We decided to wait until it was dark to give ourselves half a chance of anonymity, but the farmer spotted us, and a chase ensued. Luckily we were young and fit and could show most people a clean pair of heels, but as the chase lengthened we began to tire, and had to start dropping apples to lighten our load. The net result was that we had no apples to show for our ploy, and a trail of evidence leading straight to ourselves.

It was a highly professional setup, and chalk and cheese, in terms of size and numbers, compared to what I had been used to, growing up on the croft in Grimsay. I spent just over a year there, and enjoyed every minute of it, even though the work was hard. My biggest pay was £5 a week, which wasn't bad, and I managed to save enough to buy my first motorbike, an old BSA, which my mates used to say stood for 'bumping slowly along.' It only cost £65. Of course one of my friends had a BSA 650 Golden Flash, which was a beautiful bike, and was considered state of the art, and another had a Norton 'Dominator'. I was happy enough though. I could get from A to B, and that's what counted. You had to start somewhere.

I don't even know if you had to have a license in those days. Certainly, no one ever checked, and I never asked. I remember getting quite brave with my bike, and taking what I thought was a huge journey to Kilpatrick Flemming, which is about three or four miles from Gretna, to visit an aunty who was living there at the time. She worked in a big old folk's home. I was motoring away quite happily near a place in Perthshire called Blackford, when I must have lost concentration and skidded almost into the path of a lorry. I was lucky, as I wasn't wearing a crash helmet, and I ended up with a big hole in my head.

I spotted a tearoom as I came along the road, and was thinking about stopping for a cup of tea, and that's what must have thrown my concentration. Ironically enough, I was taken to the upstairs of that tearoom, where a nurse patched me up, and then back on the road again.

When I eventually did arrive at Kilpatrick Flemming, my aunty nearly dropped when she saw the state of me. I was still covered in blood, although it looked worse than it was.

I stayed with my aunt for a couple of days, and I visited 'Bruce's Cave', which was in the vicinity. I've often thought that Robert the Bruce must have done an awful lot of sleeping with all the caves he had.

I returned to Uist after a year at Findourie. I had an agricultural certificate and a year's dairy experience. What to do next? Like many of my generation, the government took that decision out of my hands, and on the 7th October 1954 I presented myself at Cameron Barracks, Inverness, to begin my period of two years National Service. While in Brechin, I had had to report to the Caird Hall in Dundee for a medical, which I had passed with flying colours.

Having liked the sea, I had been very keen on getting onto the MTB's (or motor torpedo boats), but whether they were being awkward, or my education was poor, they gave me an exam and I failed. Never one to be kept down for long, I decided then that the RAF would do me. The powers that be said fine, another exam, and I failed again. There was nothing for it but the army and straight into the infantry. So I said that the least they could do was put me into my local regiment the Cameron Highlanders so that I would be around some of my own folk. The powers that be agreed.

I just didn't take to the army, probably because I've always liked to be my own man. I didn't like to be told what to do and, my goodness, in the army they soon changed your tune. It was a terrible shock to the system, a lot of 'effing' and 'blinding', and square bashing. "You might have broken yer mother's heart, but you'll not break mine," was the RSM's favourite cry. Then he would prod you with his stick. If you weren't properly dressed on parade he would say, "You look like a sack of potatoes tied in the middle."

The training was pretty tough. You had to do ten weeks basic training, in which they gave you a real going over. You'd be in tears some days, and you had to march everywhere, even to the cookhouse. Sometimes, if I was hungry, I would join the queue twice, which meant a real sorting out if you got caught.

I suppose I was lucky in that I was pretty fit anyway. Up at home in Grimsay you had no choice. I was used to doing a day's work from the age of seven onwards, so the physical side of the army wasn't so bad. I can only imagine what those from a more pampered background went through though.

It was pretty exciting for all that, and again I enjoyed meeting all the boys I would be serving with. I knew one or two of them anyway, including Duncan MacLeod from North Uist, and Roddy MacDonald (Roddy Sammy) and Graham Richardson from Skye. Graham was a very good piper, and eventually went on to join the City of Glasgow police, playing in their world famous pipe band for a number of years.

After the basic training, we were sent to Pinefield camp in Elgin for a wee bit more training, before departing for our first posting.......Korea!

We were due to sail from Southhampton on the troop ship RMS Dunera (which, incidentally, was still in service up until recently, helping to transport school children all over the world). There was a rail strike on at the time though, so we sailed from York Hill quay in Glasgow instead.

It was a heck of a long journey, and on the hotter parts of the journey, it was terrible because there were so many bunks on top of one another. You were probably talking about one thousand people on board, so you only had a few inches to call your own. That was my first major voyage at sea. The journey seemed to take forever, although we did stop in Cape Town and Singapore for 'bunkers', or stores and fuel. We were all perfectly aware of where we were going and what we were going to, although we didn't feel in too much danger as most of the fighting seemed to have been done. I used to meet my friend Bill Robertson in Mallaig, who also served in Korea. He would say to me, "Och c'mon Ewen, I was there when they were needing them. You were there when they were feeding

With my friends on the 38ᵗʰ Parallel Korea 1957. I am sitting bottom left with my friend from Skye Ruaraidh Macdonald .behind me. The soldier bottom left in front of an unknown Korean soldier is John Home, son of the former Prime Minister Alec Douglas-Home.

them." This was basically correct because, by the time we got there, it was just a mopping up operation.

We were in a place called Kohema camp, very near the DMZ, the de-militarised zone. Kohema was infamous as the place where nearly a whole battalion of the 'Glorious Gloucesters' were wiped out. I have photographs of me sitting on the plaque that reads 'The 38th Parallel', near the Imjim river, which I swam over, just to create a wee bit of excitement.

Most of our work was observation. You would be left in an outpost with your rifle and your binoculars, to keep an eye on the enemy. You didn't need binoculars of course, as the North Koreans were only a stone's throw away and visible to the naked eye. They were spying on us too.

I didn't see much action or many skirmishes, although I do remember two Glaswegians shooting a couple of Koreans for stealing petrol. I was very sad about that, after all, it was only petrol. Clearly 'our boys' were in a mood to shoot and ask questions later. What a waste of life.

We served alongside New Zealanders, who turned out to be lovely people, and French Canadians, who I wasn't so struck on.

We would visit the French Canadian camp every so often, and you'd find eight or nine guys sitting round a table with bottles of beer, and each buying his own, which I found strange. Being from Scotland, we were used to a system where you at least bought your mates a beer.

I even found time in Korea to take part in a six-mile cross-country run, where I represented my battalion. The terrain was pretty hilly, which suited me, and I came in ninth out of seventy-two. My brother, Angus, was in Korea with me. We were both in the Camerons, and I often tease him that he came in nineteenth in the race. He still runs. In fact, he ran the West

Highland Way in twenty-five hours, twenty-five minutes when he was fifty-eight years old.

I'm glad to say that we both got through Korea unscathed, and after being there for about a year, we were sent home. The difference between us was that Angus liked the army. He joined on as a regular for another year after he had completed his National Service. I didn't fancy that though. I couldn't wait to get out.

On the 4th October 1956 I was demobbed. It was great to get your civilian gear on again, although I did keep my Cameron kilt as a memento. That's a wee bit illegal, but I justified it to myself by saying that the army got the two best years of my life for £3 17/- and 6d. So I kept the kilt, and recently I bought a jacket and some gear to go with it, so who knows, I may just wear it again. It still fits me after all these years.

I suppose my two-year stint in the army had a profound effect on me. It helped me to smooth some of my rougher edges, and although I am now a Jehovah's Witness, and therefore opposed to war, I believe that a year in the army would do most young folk no harm at all. It definitely teaches respect and discipline, which is no bad thing in most cases.

I had many plans for what I would do on leaving the army. I definitely had a hankering for the sea by this stage, and I planned to go to the whaling in the South Atlantic with Salvesens, because I knew this guy Peterson, who was off Shetland people and lived in Leith, which is where most of the whalers sailed from; the 'Southern Harvester' and the 'Southern Venture', factory ships like that.

There were another couple of land based jobs on offer, but I just couldn't be bothered having anything more to do with agriculture, though my father wasn't very pleased about that.

The whalers were based down about South Georgia, and then you went another two thousand miles into the ice, into

Antarctica. That really appealed to me. I definitely fancied a bit of excitement in my life, and seafaring seemed to offer that.

It would have meant being away for at least seven or eight months. That was roughly the shortest trip, which didn't bother me, as I had no real ties anyway.

It wasn't to be though. As it happened, another seed had been planted. On my way back from Korea aboard the troop ship 'Asturias', I befriended a Lewisman who was a baker aboard the vessel. He used to give me cakes and filled my head full of stories about the merchant navy, which must have been a big influence on me. I knew in my heart that as much as I wanted excitement, I desperately wanted to see a bit of the world as well, and what better way than sailing under the 'red duster.'

A Life on the Ocean Wave

It was still very common for boys from Uist to go to sea when I started, although it would have been far more common during my father's time, as there weren't many jobs other than crofting.

It's funny, but although many people complained about the army coming to Benbecula, it certainly provided jobs and greater choice of occupation in Uist.

I didn't have that choice, but then everyone else was joining the merchant navy, and I suppose that it is a bit disappointing that there are no longer so many boys from the islands or the western seaboard going to sea. We have a long maritime tradition and it is sad that that is on the wane. That, however, is the way of the world. I suppose that, as with the fishing industry, we can be our own worst enemies. When I speak to some of the young lads from Mallaig who are still deep sea, it seems that there aren't many of the older companies or lines still in existence. I certainly don't recognise many of the names.

The likes of Cunard have suffered because of the decreasing numbers of passengers still interested in travelling anywhere by sea, or even cruising for that matter. Forty years ago air travel was still in its infancy, it was still much more common to sail somewhere rather than fly. The big ocean liners were amongst the finest achievements of engineering that this country has ever produced. Speed is now the thing. You can fly to New Zealand within twenty-four hours rather than spending five weeks at sea, as was the norm previously.

Strangely enough, I don't speak on this with any great authority, as I was never in New Zealand. I was in Australia on what were known as 'tramp ships', which meant that they would pick up cargo anywhere in the world en-route to a given destination, which made for some pretty interesting, not to say mazy, journeys.

I started to notice towards the end of my time at sea that many of the crews of British vessels were becoming predominantly foreign, although the officers remained British. I include myself in the latter as I was, technically, an officer, and prided myself on the fact that the ship could not sail without me. Yes indeed, I was very important. You could sail without the captain, the chief officer would take over in the event of emergency, but you couldn't sail without a radio officer, and quite often I was the only one.

I only sailed on a few ships where there was more than one radio officer, the most notable being the Cunard liner Ivernia, which had three radio officers, but that was the exception rather than the rule.

Leaving home wasn't such a wrench, as I had already been away at school and had done my national service, and I always liked to travel. That was what really fixed it for me. I wanted to see other people and other lands; different ways of life, and I think I pretty much achieved that.

I would still like to go and see my sister Margaret in New Zealand, but I'm in no real hurry to go anywhere else, and I am getting on now. I seem to have done enough. After all, as you will read later, I did spend a year and eight days at sea on one ship, with an approximate mileage of 90,000.

Eventually I went home to Grimsay where I was employed once more on the croft, and cutting seaweed. This was never going to last though, and I was no sooner home than I was plotting my escape.

I received a grant from Inverness County Council, which enabled me to go to the James Watt College in Greenock, where I trained as a radio operator. There were three choices of certificate; PMG, which stood for Post Master General, first and second class, and also your radar ticket. I opted for the softer option of second class, because it would allow me to have a social life as well.

My interest in communications had been started in the army, where I was part of a signal platoon. This made me feel very important, although we had to do all the same drills and guard duties as the other squaddies. I recall once we were on a night patrol exercise, and the captain of the signal platoon put me in charge of the rum issue. The wrong man I can assure you. I filled my water bottle with rum, which turned out to be really powerful stuff. So powerful, in fact, that me and some of my mates got plastered. The next morning the sergeant major was not best pleased. He read the riot act to us, and we were lucky we didn't get jailed.

We learned Morse code to a fairly basic level in the army, probably only five or six words per minute, and my speed would definitely have to improve (as a PMG second class, I would be expected to send somewhere in the region of twenty words per minute) It seemed a better option though, than just going to sea and sailing as an Able Bodied seaman.

Some guys were very quick at sending messages. Some of them used what was called a 'buck key', which meant that the key moved from side to side rather than up and down. This made it a lot faster. I used to admire the concentration of some of the top boys as well. The captain would be yapping away about a telegram, they would be listening to Morse (sending and receiving) and getting involved in the captain's conversation as well. All without making a mistake. That took some doing.

Once in Greenock, if you were attending all your classes, it usually took two to three months to get up to speed. We had theory classes as well, looking at the history of morse code, and the science behind it. My problem was that I didn't like exams. I was fine at sending and receiving under normal circumstances, but if someone was examining my performance, I tended to freeze. I had to have two goes at passing the final exam.

I remember the first time fine. I had to take tranquillisers to steady my nerves and I failed, so I had to wait another two or three months before trying again. The next time I made sure that I had two big glasses of whisky inside me and I went through it no bother at all.

Angus Alec MacDonald, who had been at Balmacara with me, also attended the James Watt College at the same time. He ended up getting a fantastic shore based job with Cunard, after a few years at sea. He was a great help to me in Greenock.

I should have gone straight to sea after leaving the college but, as usual, things weren't so straightforward. The summer of 1958 found me, for some reason or other, working as a waiter in the Hydro Hotel in Pitlochry. A strange career change you may think, and I wouldn't disagree. At that time you may even have been considered slightly feminine for working as a waiter. I was the only male working alongside six females from Lewis, and they were convinced that there was something wrong with me. Sometimes they would even raid my room and attack me, which I quite enjoyed actually. Maybe I wasn't so daft.

After that, I found myself working on a flea-ridden tugboat on the Clyde. She was called the 'Flying Tempest'. That only lasted two or three weeks though, and most of that time was spent cleaning and painting her. That probably inspired me to start my next venture as a 'Clean Easy Man', a door to door salesman trying to shift cans of 'Johnson's Polish.'

You always carried a duster with you, and would demonstrate the potency of your new miracle product on the door jamb or any available space. This was always accompanied by a rich lather of patter, along the lines of, "I know your door is clean madame, but even you must admit there is a difference when I put my own polish on." I wasn't in line for any salesman of the year awards. I didn't like the job anyway. I thought it was totally stupid. I wasn't cut out for that.

I then became a plumber's mate in Scott Lithgow's shipyard, working down in the bowels of ships. It got a few pounds in, but was only really a stopgap until I settled into my chosen career as a radio operator.

I eventually found myself on the payroll of IMR (International Marine Radio), who were similar to Marconi, and I joined my first ship at the Queens Dock in Glasgow on the 13th May 1959. It was one of the Anchor-Donaldson line, and was called the 'Egidia'. I was on her for about three or four months.

We sailed for India through the Suez Canal, which was open at that time, and then I became ill in Aden, which is a hole of a place anyway. It was probably caused by dirty places, and drinking the local beer in these same dirty places. I was badly jaundiced, and it was a bad experience, as I was confined to my cabin onboard a ship without a medical officer. The Captain was expected to know a little bit about medicine, but you did wonder. I had to take my own temperature, and basically fend for myself.

Luckily there was another radio operator aboard. I was second radio officer because, being my first ship, you had to train under a chief operator until you knew how to take charge of operations yourself. You see it wasn't all sending and receiving Morse code. It was your responsibility to make sure that the radio station was 'on', especially if you were the sole radio operator on board, which I was for years. You had to do eight hours out of twenty-four with what they called the automatic alarm switched on. If someone was in distress, and sending an 'SOS', it would activate your radio set immediately. They could be fifty miles away, but you still had to go up to the shack and attend to it. There was also the possibility that it would be set off by lightning. So it was just as well that I wasn't alone, because I was so ill, that I couldn't remember a thing about the Indian Ocean, which must have taken us the best part of a week to cross, until we finally arrived in Bombay.

On arrival in Bombay, I was taken to a British run hospital called Breach Candy. It was nice and clean compared to most of Bombay. There was a swimming pool in the grounds, and I was well attended to.

I was only signed on articles on that vessel, so I wasn't actually one of the crew as such. The difference being that I was still getting paid although I was ill. I stayed there a couple of weeks, while the ship went to several other ports en route to Karachi, and by the time she came back, I was fit to sail back to the UK.

I hung around Glasgow for a while, which I quite enjoyed really, and then the next month I found another ship. I could actually have found another ship the day I got back, as there was that much work at the time.

I was still employed by IMR, and was asked to sail as a radio officer with an iron ore boat called 'Orepton'. I only did three months on her also. We were taking ore from Sept Iles, in the Gulf of St. Lawrence to Barry, or Port Talbot, in Wales, which gave me my first chance to sample the wild pubs of Tiger Bay, in Cardiff.

I signed off that boat on 16th December 1959, after several rough winter voyages on the western ocean. Especially rough with a full cargo of iron ore. We had had to avoid icebergs up in the Bering Sea, and near the Newfoundland coast. They can be very dangerous at the best of times.

It was mostly Englishmen that I had been sailing with at this point, Scousers and Cockneys. They were great seamen, but if they got drunk, they really fell out. You were better with a whole crew of Scousers or a whole crew of Londoners. They didn't mix well. Being a radio operator, I was only really supposed to socialise with officers, but I was only too happy to drink with anyone, which was definitely frowned upon. It was something to do with knowing your place.

I suppose they were right. Familiarity breeds contempt. You notice it in wee things, like stewards not cleaning your cabin properly, because 'It's only Ewen's cabin.'

By January 1960 I was back at sea again. I joined a ship called the Ivernia, owned by Cunard. This was definitely a step up, and was a posh boat compared to the ones I had been on. You definitely had to drink with the officers on Cunard's lime. You even dressed for dinner with a bow tie and cummerbund, and were expected to sit at the captain's table on occasion.

The ship was bigger and faster than I had been used to as well. It was 21,000 ton gross, and could do about 20 knots, and being a passenger liner, it meant that I was only third radio officer. I did a couple of trips from Southampton to New York, which I considered very glamorous.

My first time in New York was quite something. As a radio officer, when you hit port, you have plenty time on your hands. You're supposed to carry out maintenance work on your radio set, but I suppose I was basically lazy when it came to things like that. I just sent for the technicians, and they would sort my radio for me, which left me with plenty time to experience the delights of the 'Big Apple'.

I was a bit of a loner, so I enjoyed wandering the streets on my own, and then my imagination would get the better of me, and I'd be saying to myself, "There could be gangsters round this corner." I found my way to the Empire State building, which was just awe inspiring for a young lad from Grimsay. I decided to be awkward and have a go at climbing as many of the stairs as I could, rather than just take the easy way to the top in the elevators. I got to an observation floor near the top, where there were massive binoculars for the public's use. You could watch ships seventy or eighty miles out at sea.

I had no authority onboard that ship, being only a third radio officer. The first officer, an Englishman called Parsons, was quite strict, and he and the second radio officer both held first class radio tickets, whereas mine was only second.

I was left with the menial tasks like the typing out of the daily newsletter for the passengers. This had to be transcribed verbatim from a Morse code broadcast of world news. I found this very difficult, as I could only type with two fingers, which meant that I couldn't type as quickly as the Morse was coming in. I had to take it all down in long hand first of all, and then type it out afterwards.

I didn't last long with Cunard, although I enjoyed the trips, and was lucky enough to revisit New York on a number of occasions after that. On one trip, a friend of mine, Ian Blair, and I decided to search out a couple of beers, while our boat was docked at Bayonne, New Jersey. We were passing an American sailor's home when we saw this guy getting thrown out, quickly followed by his cases, which tumbled down the front steps after him. The sailor was shouting, "I've been at sea for the last fifty years, and I've never been treated like this," to which the fellow who was doing the throwing out replied, "I don't give a damn if you're King Neptune himself. You haven't paid up!"

Leaving Cunard wasn't really a come down, as there wasn't really much of a future in being a third radio officer anyway. I got a proper discharge of course, but they had only really taken me on for a short while anyway.

Later that year, I joined the RMS 'Caledonia', which was a cargo / passenger vessel, again belonging to the Anchor Donaldson line. She carried up to about two hundred passengers, and once more I found myself sailing for India and Pakistan.

They had two or three quartermasters aboard, one of whom was Donald Johnstone from Barra. We got on very well. I would go and visit him in his cabin, which wasn't really allowed either, as quartermasters were basically glorified ABs.

We loaded some cotton in the Sudan, which was quite a hot and dirty place, and previous to that, we went ashore in Suez, which was also quite a dirty place, but we found some pubs, and drank some French brandy, which was always good for morale.

We would always get a laugh at what we called the 'bum boats' in these places too. These were small craft that came alongside our ship trying to sell their wares, which could be anything. We would send our money down in baskets on guy ropes (you had to send the money down first) and they would send up bananas and other lovely fruit. I felt sorry for them too, as some of the more unscrupulous passengers would try and hit them with coconuts from a great height. That wasn't very nice.

There was one famous fellow on the 'bum boats' called George Robey. Everybody knew George Robey. He acquired his name from that of an English music hall star, and drew his own fame from being able to dive off his boat into the canal to retrieve shillings that people would throw to him. He was incredible. He never missed. Some cheapskates would throw a penny rather than a shilling, and George would give them hell when he reappeared from the depths. I'm sure he made a few quid.

Anyway, on this particular voyage we picked up some bales of cotton in the Sudan, and I found out that there was a bit of a watering hole, where you could get some drink, just across the river. I took a 'bum boat' across, which could be hired for pennies, or a carton of cigarettes, and enjoyed a few jars on the other side. So much so, that I had no money left to get a boat back to the other side of the river.

I would have to devise a plan quickly. I soon got hold of a boat, and began telling the boatman that I was well used to rowing, and would he mind if I had a go. He was delighted, and couldn't believe his luck, getting to sit in the back of the boat while I did all the work. Of course, he didn't know that the only reason I was doing this was because I was skint. He soon found out when we reached the other side though, and chased me all the way to the ship. He even chased me up the gangway, by which time I had been able to find a few fags to pay him with.

Again, that wasn't a terribly long voyage, probably only three months or so, as long as it would take us to get to India and back. Then it was time for another change. I don't know why I kept changing boats. Maybe I wanted to see what the rest were like. I suppose the grass was always greener on the other side of the fence.

I joined a very old Blue Star boat called the 'Seattle Star', and completed five months onboard. It was back to general cargo and twelve passengers, and me as sole radio officer, which suited me fine. It wasn't all wonderful though, because my cabin was in the base of the funnel.

We were sailing to the West Coast of America, calling at various different places along the way, like Madeira (for bunkers) and Cristobal, to gain entry to the Panama Canal, which I thought was a fantastic bit of engineering, compared to the Suez Canal. There were small locomotive engines on either side of the canal, which pulled the ship along. I don't think we were allowed to use the ship's engines.

Making port was also an opportunity to receive mail, which became very important when you were deep sea. Letters seemed to take on more importance when you were far from home. Most decent companies had a head office where mail could be sent. Many of these tended to be based in Leadenhall Street in London. You gave your folks or loved ones the name of your boat (hopefully they knew your own name), care of the London office, and they would send any mail in good time to the port you were sailing for at that time. They always knew the whereabouts of the vessel, because if they didn't, I wasn't doing my job properly.

You see, I used to have to take DF, or direction finding bearings. On your radio you had what they called a direction finder, and of course they card at 360°. You would have a book telling you where the principal DF stations were, and the captain would tell you, in relation to your own position, to take a bearing. You usually had to take three, all 90°, away from each other, and this would give you a better idea of your own position. This also works for visual bearings too.

We used huge radios with valves, which are now pretty much obsolete, and an emergency set, in case your radio went on the blink. Many of the older ships only had 150-watt radios, which made it difficult sending messages home if you were a long way from the UK. You were forced to use the ionosphere, or Appleton Layer, at certain times of the day and night to help bounce the signal back to the main station at Portishead, near Bristol. Portishead was one of the most famous names in maritime communications, until it closed in 2000. There were about fifteen different stations around Britain when I was at sea, so the chances were that somebody would hear you.

It could be a stressful job at times, especially if the station you were trying to send to was busy. I've seen it take as much as eleven or twelve hours to get a telegram through if things were flat out, or you had bad equipment or a bad reception. People would say, "och, a radio operator? Clean hands!" but it could be a big responsibility, and sometimes you were a bag of nerves. You had to be on the ball twenty-four hours a day, and mistakes certainly weren't tolerated.

We called at many ports on America's Pacific coast on our way to Vancouver, in Canada. I remember some of the names like San Pedro, in Long Beach California, which was one of the principal harbours in the Los Angeles area. We also went to San Francisco, Eureka, Seattle and Portland (Oregon), which was a lovely place.

I liked San Francisco too, even though I got myself in a bit of trouble with a big coloured chap. As usual, there was drink involved, and I'd gone outside with the guy, accompanied by two big Englishmen who I thought were going to give me a hand to 'duff him up'. The tables fairly turned though, when several other coloured guys appeared on the scene, and the upshot was that I got seriously hammered. I was lucky because I could have been thrown in the harbour, and so much for the radio operator then.

The next morning I was up before the captain, who gave me a real dressing down, and no wonder. Even an AB doing that would have been just not on. Anyway, I lived to tell the tale.

Looking back, I wonder now if the captain was maybe an 'Alcoholics Anonymous' man himself. Maybe he could see the beginnings of a problem in me.

Another time he sent two cadets up to get a hold of the bold Ewen, who was socialising in a pub and talking bullshit as usual. I took umbrage at the fact that the captain had only sent cadets to summon me, and soon told them that I would go back to the ship when I was good and ready. I was playing on the assumption that the ship couldn't sail without me, which really maddened the skipper.

When I eventually decided to make my way back, I was in a mood for showing off. I jumped onto the safety net below the gangway, and climbed hand over hand onto the ship. Once onboard, I then decided to go for a walk along the belting of the boat, to show how sober I was. I wouldn't have dreamt of attempting that if I had been sober.

On meeting the captain, he handed some telegrams that had to be sent to Vancouver. Suddenly there was a gale of wind, and I was that drunk that the telegrams blew away, and maybe they made it to Vancouver under their own steam, who knows? That was the final straw. The captain chased me to my cabin, and the next morning he read the riot act to me, telling me in no uncertain terms that I would receive no 'sub', and I would not be allowed ashore when we reached Vancouver, which hit me hard, as I had relations there that I was keen to see.

He was a good man though. He could have chosen to put a bad mark in my book, but instead he forgave me, and I behaved myself for the rest of the voyage.

I had a great time ashore in Vancouver. I visited all my relations, some of whom lived in Quebec Street, and one of my Skye relations, Kenny Campbell, who owned two hotels in the city at that time, one called the Metropol and one called the Ambassador. He lived in a posh area of Vancouver called English Bay.

My relations, in Vancouver, were great people for going and visiting one another, and were very hospitable, most of them anyway. There was one old cousin whose wife didn't like Highland people, and it got quite embarrassing for the poor man, as we got hardly even a bite to eat. As we left the house, I can remember pretending to tighten my belt, and saying to one of my other relations, "By God, that was some feed in there."

On another occasion I was looking for a friend from North Uist who lives in New Westminster. I saw this huge man and I asked him directions. He turned to me and said, "A bheil Gaidhlig agad?" "Do you have Gaelic?" I was stunned, but only too happy to converse in our first language. It turned out that he was a distant relation of mine also. Not only that, but he was a millionaire who had made his money in bootlegging or 'rum running,' during the prohibition era. I'll not say his name in English, but he was known back home as Ruaridh Tearlach. He was a very kind man, and invited me back to his house, and showed me where Angus MacLean, who had come from Benbecula, stayed. They were quite a well to do family also. Angus was known in Uist as 'Aonghas a' Phleasdair', and came from Church Hill in Griminish. He had relatives who did really well in the Government of Rhodesia, when Ian Smith was in power.

There was a large community of Highland exiles in Vancouver and I found them, on the whole, a very kind and welcoming people. They seemed to have kept alive the old ceilidh traditions, maybe even better than we did back home.

I still have relations there, who live in North Vancouver. They're over eighty now, but I still phone them and keep in touch as best I can.

It's a good job I was allowed ashore, as I would have missed out on the experience of a lifetime and, if you know anything about the Highlands, you can be sure that news of my misdemeanour would have reached home before I did, had I been confined to quarters.

I came home from that trip in December 1960, and I was away again on the 23rd January 1961, signed on a boat called the 'Denby Grange', which was owned by a company called Holder Brothers. They had a fleet of cargo and passenger boats.

It was aboard the 'Denby Grange' that I first sailed with my mate Ian Blair. I'm glad to say that I'm still mates with him. I had known Ian before, because when my brother John was ill, Ian's mother took him in between hospital appointments, which was very kind of her, and a bond grew between both families.

Myself and Ian used to get up to some terrible mischief while at sea. I still keep in contact with him. He lives up in Spinningdale in Easter Ross. We were once anchored off the Italian coast, near the port of La Spezia, and took it upon ourselves to be the first to port by swimming ashore, the distance being about three quarters of a mile. We were joined on our escapade by another chap who was also keen on being one of the first of our crew ashore in Italy.

Both the other two boys were strong swimmers, very adept at the front crawl, whereas I could only really swim a couple of hundred yards doing the breast stroke, which became very tiring after a while. It was all a bit daft, though nothing compared to the stunt pulled by a guy I sailed with on another ship. He dived off the vessel, swam under her, and came up on the other side, which was very stupid. I would never have considered that, not even in my madder days.

Anyway, we jumped off the ship in our swimming trunks and, by hook or by crook, we made it ashore, which was an achievement of sorts. Drunk on the success of our venture, we decided to swim back, and that is when our problems started. I got a terrible cramp in my left leg, which was quite painful, so I had to take a rest on my back, and just do the best I could, while the strongest swimmer of the other two swam to get help.

When he reached the ship, the chief officer refused to lower the lifeboat, saying that we had no business being ashore in the first place. The poor guy had no option but to swim back to us and, as he said himself, "You'll just have to survive Mac."

When we did eventually make it to the ship, the rest of the crew clearly felt sorry for us and threw life belts and life jackets, which posed their own problems as they were made of much harder material in those days and could easily have knocked us out. I was kind of determined by that stage, ignoring the life belts, and just swam for the ladder, which I began to climb in foul humour.

I didn't realise just how hard a thirty-five foot perpendicular climb was going to be after my exertions though. My arms and legs refused to work properly, and my muscles burned in every sinew as I clung to that ladder for dear life. Believe you me, it was a very relieved Ewen Nicholson that finally scrambled over the gang rail.

Never underestimate the healing ability of the human body however. After a cup of hot milk and a couple of hours kip I was as right as rain and raring to go again. I never did bother having it out with the chief officer, but then, he wasn't exactly what you might call the most approachable of men.Ian was fourth engineer, which I think he sailed as all his life. Him and I got on great, and were together on that ship for over eight months. We visited a lot of places during that time. We were in Singapore and the Persian Gulf, and were also in Borneo, in a place called Balikpapan. Again, we found drink, which was something I became highly adept at. The trouble was though, in this case, we fancied trying some of the home made 'jungle juice', and, by God, we got it.

I wouldn't quite say headhunter territory, but it wasn't far off it. Officially, you couldn't get any alcohol apart from beer, but the locals used to make this bad concoction, which they would produce for the more hardened drinkers amongst us. No prizes for guessing that I was at the head of the queue, and drank far more of the stuff than I should have done. We found ourselves in a fairly shifty looking honky tonk, with a few women spread about the place. They kept the stuff, which I would imagine was totally illegal, under their skirts.

Returning to the ship, we were both well oiled, and walking along the fly bridge of the boat. I was talking to the chief officer, and twirling the keys to my cabin round on my finger, when they dropped about thirty feet down. In my attempt to rescue them quickly, I missed my footing and also fell thirty feet, leaving my head badly injured.

On being taken ashore, we found that there was no proper doctor to be found, so my head was just held together with very strong elastic plaster. I don't know sometimes how I'm still here.

I was very bad for attacking my own head, especially on that ship. We had a small swimming pool onboard, and one day we were celebrating what we called 'Crossing the Line'. This was when you went over 180° longitude, and crossed the International Date Line. You always had a celebration onboard a ship that crossed the line, especially if there were people

72

onboard who had never done it before. I went for a swim, which I liked doing in the tropics, although I couldn't have been very good at diving, as I jumped in and split my head on the bottom of the pool. I certainly couldn't be accused of sparing myself.

I managed to get some sort of medical attention, a bandage or something, but certainly not the sort of attention that a gash like that merited. There was definitely no doctor on board. The captain had a great laugh about it "Hey, Marconi," he said, "make sure there's some water in the pool the next time you jump in."

I signed off the 'Denby Grange', and left the Holder Brothers Shipping Company in September 1961. In October I took a Blue Star boat from Liverpool round to London, which was only two or three days, and must have been one of my shortest trips. It didn't matter how short the trip though, they still had to have a radio operator onboard.

I was definitely suffering itchy feet though, and decided that, for the time being, I'd had enough of seeing the world through a porthole.

The Call of the Second City

I was paid off in September 1961, and headed back to Glasgow. I had a definite attraction to the second city of the Empire. I enjoyed the social life; the dancing and the choice of pubs that you had. Pubs in Glasgow intrigued me. If I heard that such and such a pub was quite a tough place, then I always went and had a look, although I was crafty enough never to stay too long. I always found my way about Glasgow according to pub names.

The Saracen's Head, or 'Sarry Heid', as locals knew it, on the Gallowgate was a favourite. They drank scrumpy in there, which was pretty much unheard of elsewhere. It was one of the roughest pubs in the city, and I'm pretty sure that it was owned by a Lewis or Harrisman at the time. There was certainly a bouncer from the islands on the door who spotted me a mile off. "You look kind of Heiland", he said. "What the hell are you doing in here?"

"Och, I'm just here to sample your scrumpy," says I.

I gave him my money, he being such a big chap that he was able to reach over the heads of the crowd to get my pint, which I settled down to drink. After a while, I went to the toilet where I was button-holed by this wee bachle who had noticed that I wasn't regular, and I took that as my cue to get out of there. So off I went, across the road to the world famous 'Barrowland Ballroom', to a dance. They missed nothing, although if you behaved yourself, nobody bothered you, so maybe their reputation was undeserved.

My Uncle Angus was only in Glasgow once, during a spell in hospital. During his stay, my brother took him to a couple of 'rough pubs' in Maryhill. When my brother asked Angus what he thought, my uncle replied, "Oh here, they're no any worse than Creagorry, for the amount of people that are in them."

I decided a spell ashore might suit me, and actually began working as a barman myself. I started with an Aberdonian called David Ross, who had a pub called the Pittodrie Bar on the corner of West Nile Street and Cowcaddens. I was second in command, which meant I had to carry out cellar duties as well. I enjoyed it very much though. The pub had quite a respectable clientele, and you weren't allowed to serve anyone who'd had too much of the wine.

There was a big policeman whose beat covered the area that the pub was in, and he always came in for a big glass of whisky. Whether he was on duty or not, it didn't matter, he just liked his glass of whisky. One morning I was asked to go and open the pub, as the charge hand was off, and I lived at George's Cross. On my arrival, I found that the windows of the pub had been smashed with a bit of railing, which was still sticking out of one of them, so off I went to find the big policeman, to see if he could help at all. "Never saw a thing," he said. He didn't want to get involved. He was more interested in his big glass of whisky.

I stayed in the pub trade for a couple of years, moving on to the Lorn Bar, in St. Enoch Square, where I worked alongside a charge hand called MacKinnon, who hailed from Skye. I suppose, looking back, I was well down the road to being an alcoholic by this stage, but I worked alongside a guy who was even further down the road than me, wee Joe, who was the father of the famous singer Lena Martell.

I never drank while I was on duty. I was always able to control that, because I knew that if I took one, I would take more. A very good friend told me that the smell of one could be the smell of ten, so I just didn't bother when I was working. Although, I was probably the bar's best customer when I wasn't.

Of course, this is me being wise with the benefit of hindsight, and after twelve years of sobriety. I didn't realise I had a problem then, but it creeps up on you like any illness. And that's what it is, an illness, and a bad one at that.

I didn't miss going to sea during that time, and I knew that when I was ready for it, I would go back. By 1963 I felt I was ready, and joined a ship in September of that year. I stayed aboard the 'Petalon', as she was named, until June of the following year. I can't remember exactly where we sailed to, although I must of racked up another couple of the forty-eight or forty-nine countries I visited whilst at sea.

I went home to Uist for a while after that, and reacquainted myself with life and work on the family croft, which was good for me, and good for the soul for a little while. Soon, however, the bright lights were beckoning again, and I found myself a job with a team of Irish navvies, digging up the streets of Glasgow and laying cables for a firm called British Insulated Callender's Cable Ltd.

I was different from your average radio operator. You weren't supposed to be seen with a pick or shovel in your hand, but that didn't bother me. I was often glad of the change, variety being the spice of life. The sea would always pull me back, but I didn't believe that it should necessarily have the monopoly on my life. I enjoyed a change and a different challenge now and again.

I enjoyed going to sea, but, at times, I preferred the shore life, which may strike you as odd. I found cities like Glasgow fascinating, which was maybe unusual for someone from such a rural background. I don't know. I suppose I was always different.

I enjoyed London too. There was a quaint little pub on the Thames called the Prospect of Whitby, which stood near Wapping tube station. It went back well over three hundred years, and had been a favourite haunt of smugglers and bootleggers. Maybe that is why I enjoyed it so much. It was a great place to watch the shipping going up and down the river.

I danced at the Hammersmith Palace as well, and have very fond memories of it. As I said, I was a bit of a loner, and took terrible chances going round some of these places, but when you are young, you are invincible, especially with the shield of alcohol by your side.

London was such a huge place compared to Glasgow. You could travel round it for a hundred and fifty years and still not know it but, of course, Glasgow had a large Highland community which London didn't.

Most guys who are at sea get itchy feet when they are at home for any length of time, but the only itchy feet I would get was when the money ran out.

I earned quite good money as a labourer, which helped to augment my drinking, so that always helped me to stay ashore, otherwise I would have gone back quicker. I loved the social whirl of Glasgow, dances in Govan Town Hall, and at the Highlander's Institute in Elmbank Street. It was all massively appealing to a young single man.

My brother found a picture of me dancing in the Albert Ballroom about 1962, in a newspaper in Glasgow last year. I have a photo of it somewhere. I wasn't there often, but maybe the old Highlander's Institute in Elmbank Street was full that night. I had to laugh at the caption below the photo. It said 'maybe the man in the blazer turned up at the wrong night.' Sure enough, there I was in my blazer surrounded by women in mini-skirts, and I was dancing with one, who had hardly a pelmet on. I was a member of the SNP at the time and it looks like their blazer, or possibly that of the wireless college in Greenock, that I'm wearing.

Anyway, back to the day job. To get work with that particular team of navvies you were advised to go and see the gaffer, either in Doyle's pub in the Gorbals, or the 'Barras' market on a Sunday. He would either tell you to clear off or turn up the next day to see what you could do and, by God, you had to work hard with the pick and shovel. He would show you a trench in the morning, and you were expected to get down there and not reappear until the end of the day. He would say to you, "I want to see plenty muck coming up all day, and you coming up in the evening. And if it's too deep a hole to get out of, just build yourself steps to climb out."

The gaffer would be on a bonus for finishing any job early, and I remember him working us particularly hard on a job where we were laying 33Kv cable. There were about twenty or thirty of us pulling it off a big roll, and laying it in the trench by hand, when we decided to have a tea break. They were well organised as a gang of workers, and had an old retired man that made their tea. He would collect money off you to go and buy rolls, and make a brew.

Anyway, we left two guys in the trench to continue digging. One was on the jackhammer and one had a shovel. When we came back after our break, all we could see was the head of one of the boys peeping out over the top of the trench. The whole thing had caved in on them, because, in our efforts to get the job done quickly, we had put no proper shoring in. Both men were lucky not to have lost their lives.

On another occasion, the man that was operating the jackhammer put it through a mains cable and died instantly from electrocution. Life was cheap with these boys. Nobody got sued; it was just back on with the job. Nobody was irreplaceable.

We called the gaffer, who was a wee stout man, 'Dublin.' He was as hard as nails, and stayed in London Road with his family. He used to shout sometimes, "There'll be changes here boys, and I don't mean in the weather. If you don't work harder, there'll be new faces tomorrow." And he would mean it. He would sack you if you didn't graft.

These boys played hard as well. They liked their Guiness, and could easily knock back ten pints in a single sitting no bother. They were hard times, but good times, and I enjoyed the comradeship. I was sorry to leave, but felt that I had to move on.

Next up was a job with BRS (British Road Services), in their parcel department, in Portman Street in Govan. You had to distribute parcels from different lorries and destinations. You had a wee bogey with which you travelled the depot putting the relevant parcels in the relevant sections.

Unfortunately, my work for BRS was interrupted by two months ill health. In fact, I should really come clean, I got into another fight, and got my nose broken again, so I decided to get it mended properly in Stobhill Hospital. That accounted for my two-month absence.

You might think I was quite handy with the mitts, but this wasn't the case at all, although maybe I could have been, if I had received some proper training. It was always drink fuelled with me, and there were always just two hits; them hitting me, and me hitting the deck.

It was time to go back to sea.

Farewell to the Tail of the Bank

On board a Greek Ship in the 60's

In December 1965 I joined a Greek ship called 'Nicolaos Embiricos', which was owned by the Embiricos family, and carried a general cargo.

Mr Embiricos was a multi-millionaire, and owned a private yacht called 'Astarte', which I was soon transferred to. That suited me just great, because he was an awful nice chap, and we were always ashore socialising. Mind you, it was useless for saving any money.

The yacht was just used for personal cruising, and must have been quite a big one, as it had a crew of twenty-one. We travelled all over the Mediterranean and were based in a place called Vouliagmeni, which is about ten miles south of Piraeus. We would visit Crete and many of the islands around there, including Gavdos, which is the southernmost of all the Greek islands.

The chief steward was an Italian by the name of Luigi, who ensured that we always had good food. There was always champagne and caviar, and Mr Embiricos and his wife, or his girlfriend (or maybe somebody else's wife) used to have big parties aboard, which seemed to last for days. His party trick was to throw empty bottles of wine up in the air, and see if he could blast them with his shotgun.

The best place we ever visited, although it was very expensive, as we were trying to live like millionaires for a day, was Venice. San Marco's Square really stuck in my mind, and we visited a pub there called Charlie's Bar, where royalty used to hang out, and the prices reflected this. We had a couple of trips on the gondolas, and went by speedboat to the world famous Lido Beach.

I certainly wouldn't have got bored of life onboard the Astarte, in fact I had developed a taste for the high life. The problem was that I just wasn't saving any money. I decided I would have to go back to doing longer trips, where there wasn't the possibility of visiting so many ports.

To that end, I joined one of Mr Embiricos' cargo boats, called 'Eugenie Embiricos', and did quite a long voyage on that. Well, actually, I should have done a long voyage, but I took terribly ill in Costa Rica, and was advised by the shore doctor to sign off, because I had infective hepatitis. Very serious stuff. Again, the horrible, dirty places that I always chose to drink in had done for me.

I was the only radio officer onboard, and we were en route to Yokohama, which was one month across the Pacific. For this reason, the captain wasn't keen on me signing off the ship, and said to me, "Oh you're hardy, you're Scots. You'll make it no bother. I'll sign you off myself when we get to Yokohama." I replied, "I might no be alive by the time we reach Yokohama."

We eventually compromised, and reached a gentleman's agreement, whereby he would put me ashore when we reached Hawaii, which was half way across the Pacific. There was no doctor onboard, so I was basically confined to the radio room on my own for the two-week journey, and all I had to eat in that fortnight was two very thin bowls of chicken soup. I was never a very big man, but I lost a stone and a half. I was desperately ill, although the captain would tell me everyday that I was looking much better. He was only worried about whether or not the propeller was turning.

We were lucky that the weather was fine, as I wasn't able to send any messages during the two weeks, apart from a quick line to head office in London to send a relief radio officer to Honolulu ASAP. It really all boiled down to the old problem that a ship couldn't sail without a radio officer.

The conflict in Vietnam was at its peak at that time and Hawaii was awash with American military personnel. I was eventually checked over by an American medical officer, who reckoned there was no doubt about the fact that I had hepatitis, and all the symptoms; yellow eyes, and under my tongue was all yellow. I was taken to the Queen Mother Hospital, which was a lovely, clean, American run establishment, and was put in an isolation ward immediately.

As fate would have it, I still had my wee button accordion that I had bought in Albany, Australia, with me, so that helped to pass the time when I was feeling a little better.

I was put on a special diet, and I did start to regain my strength, although the head doctor warned me never to touch alcohol ever again. He reckoned that cirrhosis of the liver could set in pretty quick as a result of the hepatitis, if I was ever to imbibe again. As it happened, I was feeling too ill to even think about drink.

After two or three weeks, I was flown to London via San Francisco and Kennedy Airport, New York, and came home to Glasgow in May 1967 to try and recover fully. At least that was the idea, but I found myself working in pubs again, and drinking sherry, which I convinced myself wasn't really alcohol.

By this time I had bought myself a wee room and kitchen in Govan. The thought of owning my own part of the red sandstone building made me feel quite important. I even had an inside toilet, or 'cludgie,' as they call it in Glasgow. It was a nice wee flat, and when I was at sea, I would rent it out.

I still tell people, when they find out that I lived in Govan, that I sold my flat to Rab C. Nesbitt, and my string vest as well.

I then went home for another spell, which was always a good bolthole if I found myself unemployed. I would cut seaweed for Alginate Industries, and my father still had a wee boat with an engine, with which we fished creels.

If you found a good area, the seaweed was incredibly plentiful. You had to put a rope around it, before the tide came in, and then you had to tow it with your boat. You had to be very accurate with your towing, as you could be towing for anything up to two miles. You had to know your tides and currents, and eventually you beached it on the sand over at Gramsdale, where the lorries would come and get it for the factory in South Uist.

I was able to cut several tons of seaweed in a day, and that was before the days of forklifts and automation. You had to load the back of the lorry from the beach with nothing fancier than a garden rake and, once the lorry was loaded, you might even think of cutting some more. It was hard, hard work.

My sojourns at home never really lasted terribly long though. Just long enough for me to get my head and my financial situation together, and then I was off again.

In October 1967, I joined another Greek ship, although this time a tanker called 'Hydroussa'. It wasn't very big as tankers go, coming in around the twenty to thirty thousand ton mark.

Once at sea, this Russian fellow and myself were on deck together, and being slightly bored, we decided to have a test of strength, to relieve the tedium. We opted for a game of peanuts, where you grip your opponent's fingers in an interlocking fashion with your own, and try and bend them back until your opponent submits.

Your opponent doesn't always submit of course, and this fellow certainly didn't know the meaning of defeat. In fact, he didn't know the meaning of stop either, and ended up breaking my fingers. I had a stookie put on my injured hand, which is not ideal for a radio operator. A Russian doctor, who had no English, fitted the cast on my right hand, and wrote on it the date of when I could safely remove it. Needless to say, it didn't last the course, as I was having problems raising my glass in Glasgow one night, and the stookie ended up in the street.

I was ashore a couple of times behind the Iron Curtain, as it was in those days. One of my first ocean going voyages saw me ashore in Poland, where we were collecting a cargo of iron ingots to take to North Korea. The communist countries always worked very closely together, and it was almost like a secret trade that nobody in the west, apart from merchant seamen, knew about.

On another trip, my ship landed in Kherson, in what is now the Ukraine. We arrived there by way of Istanbul and the Bosphorus, before crossing the Black Sea. It was part of the Soviet Union, and regulations were very tight when we docked to pick up our cargo.

Our cargo, incidentally, was a load of Russian made tractors and diggers that we were to transport to Cuba and Fidel Castro. That was a terrible voyage. I boarded the ship in Genoa and, had it been Glasgow, I wouldn't have even bothered opening my case, it was that dirty and flea ridden. The boat sailed under a Maltese flag, so it must have been just after they gained their independence from Britain.

We had a terrible riff raff of a crew. Nobody in their right mind would have employed them, gangsters to a man. Real rough necks from Latvia, Romania and Italy, guys that wouldn't have got a job anywhere else. The owners must have been desperate for the ship to sail. The whole voyage was supposed to take two or three months, by the time we would get across the Black Sea, load our cargo and head for Cuba. I decided to tough it out.

What a mistake that was. Every misfortune that could have befallen us came our way, including mutiny. There were only three of us who sided with the captain, and we were soon told by the rest of the crew that it would be wiser to side with them. The dispute arose over the fact that the crew were wanting overtime, and I wouldn't have paid them a penny anyway. The skipper refused to give them their demands, as they weren't a good lot anyway.

Then the dispute started to get out of hand. On our way across the Atlantic, one of the guys who had sided with the captain came up from the engine room with a terrible head wound. One of the crew had put a spanner right into his head, so I had to lock my cabin door.

When we eventually landed in Matansis, in Cuba, the skipper asked me to go and see the British Consul, as we still had eighty miles to go before we reached Havana. That suggests that maybe Britain still had something to do with Malta, I don't know.

Now Cuba was quite a sensitive place at that time. The quayside was lined with soldiers armed with rifles, and the harbour was full of communist ships from various eastern bloc countries. You had to be careful getting involved in any kind of dispute, especially anything that could have diplomatic or political undertones. It was an awful job even getting to the consulate, as every bus seemed to be chock full of hens and chickens.

Anyway, I met the consul, who was a big, stout woman from England, and she was quite a firebrand. She came to the boat with a couple of officials for face-to-face talks with the crew, and there was a lot of shouting, and a fairly menacing atmosphere.

The consul decided that it would be safer for the skipper to be paid off and leave the ship, and we had to wait for this tough Italian skipper who arrived and really sorted them out.

I certainly wasn't looking forward to the return journey though. You had to watch your back, because these cutthroats didn't forget that you had sided against them, and they knew how to hold a grudge. Maybe they cut me a bit of slack because I was the radioman, and after all, everyone kind of depended on me.

I'm glad to say that we all made it back in one piece. However, when we reached port in Italy, there were police waiting for us, and the mutineers were thrown straight into jail. I was just happy to pay off and make my way home back to the UK, on the Orient Express no less. What a penance!

In April 1969 I joined a Greek ship called the 'Brimas', and that was the start of the longest trip I ever sailed on. As I told you, it lasted a year and eight days, to be exact. We went to many, many countries including Australia, Indonesia and India. It was a long time to be at sea, although we got plenty shore leave as well.

When we went into port, as a radio officer, I was often the first man ashore and the last man back onboard. If we were in for a day, then I got one day's leave, and if it was three weeks, it was three weeks. It depended on how much cargo you were loading or unloading. If you were on a tanker though, you got hardly any shore leave at all, as it was all installations and terminals you were visiting.

For the most part though, I enjoyed the places I visited. I loved Japan, and it doesn't take a lot to understand why; the saki and the women, etc. I actually fell in love with the place during my national service in Korea, when we were flown to Japan for some rest and recuperation, although there wasn't much of that, as I'm sure you can imagine.

We were flown to a beautiful wee Island near Kure called Miyajima. It was very picturesque, just as you see on the television; lovely little bridges and floral gardens.

I loved the people. They couldn't do enough for you. A sea change from the way they had behaved during the war, but I suppose even then they were a very brave people. I found the men and women incredibly nice, especially the women, although I suppose, for many of them, that was their job, entertaining in pubs and so on.

It was fairly westernised by the time I went there. I suppose there was no holding them back after Commander Perry landed in Okinawa in 1854, and, in many ways, conditions would have improved for the ordinary people, although progress is always a double edged sword, and maybe being part of a marginalised culture and growing up with English as my second language made me more aware of that.

I remember once joining a ship in Yokohama, sailing to London, then flying to Moscow and then onto Japan by Japanese Airlines across Siberia. Japan was one of the few countries in the world that would have been allowed to fly across Siberia at that time, and it was quite a trip back to Yokohama, where I joined up with another ship.

In fact, my father was onboard a ship in Yokohama Bay in 1923 when the big earthquake struck. Over 120,000 people were killed and dad was thrown out of his bunk by the force of the waves crashing off the ship.

He had a few near ones. On New Year's Eve 1919, my father was standing on the pier in Kyle of Lochalsh, waiting to get home after his military service in the first war. He very nearly sailed on the 'MV Iolaire,' onboard which, somewhere in the region of one hundred and twenty young men would perish later that night, as the vessel ran aground within sight of Stornoway harbour. He was very lucky and opted instead for a small cargo vessel called the 'Sheila,' which was making for

North Uist and Harris. His decision almost certainly saved his life.

As you have read, I loved Vancouver too. It seemed to me that the people I met there were more Scottish or more Highland than we were. It wasn't the same as every other place where you just went to a bar and got drunk. You had a wee drink with them, nice company, nice food, what more could you ask for. I have many happy memories, and photos, of my relatives in Vancouver.

They were always keen to get news from home, and I suppose, in truth, the chord never really severs. I was only too happy to oblige, as that was one of my unofficial duties onboard anyway, what with one ear constantly on the BBC World Service, I was always able to keep my shipmates abreast of current and world affairs.

I toured about a fair bit in Canada, travelling to New Westminster to visit a family called Orr. Their people had a big house in Benbecula where the doctor lives now, I think. There was a family of MacLeans as well whom I visited, and they had done very well, proving themselves to be very clever people in the process. All these people were very kind to me, and although I still had my drinking, they looked after me and made sure that my socialising never got out of hand.

I enjoyed Australia also, and it was in Albany, Western Australia that I bought my melodeon, one of the more worthwhile trinkets I picked up on my travels. I saw black swans in Perth and saw the 'garden city of Australia'. Adelaide, passing Kangaroo Island and places like that on the way to Port Lincoln. To this day I still receive a letter from relatives I was lucky enough to meet there. It's always interesting to see how things are going for them.

The patriarch of the family was an old man by the time I met them. Although he had a Highland name (Robertson) he was a proud Englishman. He was an interesting character who had a profound dislike for people who arrived in Australia and expected to make their fortune immediately and with very little effort.

He had arrived forty years previously when the passage cost a halfpenny a mile (that's a journey of approximately 10,000 miles, so work it out for yourself) and had only succeeded by the sweat of his brow and sheer grit and determination. His wife was a lovely woman who lived into her nineties, dying only a few months ago, which I was sorry to hear about.

The family still keep in touch and one or two of them have visited me in Mallaig, which has been a nice thing, After all, it is much nicer to have friends like that rather than mere acquaintances, and I suppose my years at sea allowed me that opportunity, which I am grateful for. In fact, I'm blessed because as a drinker I've seen the other side of the coin, where I had to buy my friendships in a bar, and these relationships are not of the lasting kind. You certainly couldn't rely on that kind of friendship when the chips are down.

Of course, it wasn't every place I visited that I would be desperate to go back to. There were creeks in West Africa where you would go for iron ore that filled me with dread. You certainly wouldn't go ashore, and if you did, you might never be seen again. The danger levels in any given location always seemed to be linked directly to the poverty level. The more desperate people are, the further they will go just to survive, and if that survival comes at your expense, so be it. That, I suppose, is one of the fundamental laws of nature.

India was another country that made a lasting impression on me, because of the terrible poverty I saw there. I used to steal food from the galley to feed children who seemed to live on the quayside. Each morning there would be anywhere between twelve and twenty of these poor wee souls waiting to receive any kind of nourishment. It may sound incredible, but some of these children had had limbs broken by their parents to make them look more pathetic. It became a warped sort of meal ticket. We complain in Britain, but, in all honesty, we don't know we're living.

I wasn't too keen on many of the oil terminals I visited in the Persian Gulf either. It wasn't that they were dangerous places, or impoverished, because they weren't, just deathly boring! As sailors, we liked a town with a bit of night life; dancing and women and bright lights, and unfortunately, oil terminals in the Middle East very rarely provided that opportunity. You certainly saved money on the tankers, but your social life definitely suffered, and as every young buck knows, there's more to life than making money. Mind you, Bahrain was quite nice, so it can't have been completely bad, and I suppose it all adds to the human experience.

There was many a time I would have been glad of the tedium of an Arab oil terminal though, when being buffeted in the teeth of a force ten gale or other similarly vicious weather conditions. Even in this day and age, the life of a sailor can be a particularly dangerous one (freak weather conditions are no respecter of modern safety technology), and there were often occasions when I feared for my life while battling the elements at sea.

I was on a Greek ship heading towards Hong Kong once. We were in the South China Sea with the Philippines on the starboard side in hurricane conditions. We were nearly driven ashore on more than one occasion, and it certainly didn't fill me with confidence to know that the captain had already lost two ships in similar circumstances.

To make matters worse, my radio set was hanging in bits; just a jumble of wires and circuits. It worked, but only just, and I wasn't too sure that it was going to stay working for very much longer.

While all this was happening, the captain, who seemed wholly unperturbed by the weather, was busy regaling me with the story of what happened when he lost the second of the two ships he had run aground in similar conditions. It seems they had foundered off Hinan Island, and by the grace of God, the entire crew was rescued by the islanders, many of whom had risked their own lives by throwing themselves into the sea to drag the stricken sailors ashore.

Back on dry land, the crew were picked up by the Chinese authorities and taken before a public audience in what was known as the 'Hall of the People.' The authorities were determined to turn the episode into a communist PR coup, and immediately began to question the captain about the sinking of his vessel and subsequent rescue.

The first question the beleaguered officer was asked was who or what did he think had saved the lives of him and his men, the exchange being conducted through a translator. Not wishing to give a convoluted answer, which would have to be converted to Chinese, and being a God-fearing Greek, the captain raised his right index finger skyward to indicate his belief in the intervention of the Almighty.

However, without realising it, he inadvertently pointed towards a colossal portrait of Chairman Mao Tse Tung, which brought the entire hall to its feet amidst rapturous applause. It seems the captain and his crew enjoyed the finest hospitality the Chinese had to offer after his unintended conversion to communism. It couldn't have worked out better.

Communist countries were always a little strange, to put it mildly. On another Greek ship, we sailed for North Korea (possibly the most communist of communist countries) via Shanghai, which itself was quite a town, with a population of near enough 20,000,000 even then.

The communist authorities in Shanghai monitored us very closely. When ashore, we were not really allowed outwith the confines of the Seamen's Mission. This was fair enough, but it made for a very dull period of shore leave. The only diversion was a shop in the mission, which sold everything from anchors to bicycles. I bought an air rifle (I still can't think why), but, of course, I wasn't allowed to take possession of it until the day we sailed, just in case I started my own personal armed revolt against the People's Republic. It's incredible to think of it now, but they really were that paranoid.

There was a cook on a British vessel that had a talent for drawing cartoons and caricatures. He was forever drawing comic sketches of his shipmates and officers, and had even drawn a small picture lampooning Mau Tse Tung, which hung in the galley. Apparently, this was noticed by one of the communist party members who were forever snooping around foreign ships, and on his next visit ashore, the cook disappeared and was never seen again. Events in Shanghai, however, would soon pale into insignificance compared to what awaited us at our journey's end.

North Korea made China look positively liberal. It was quite simply the most hard-line state I ever visited, and was still ruled by the iron fist of Kim Il-Sung. I remember it being exceptionally cold when we arrived (I don't recall the name of the port) and we were met by one of the ship's Korean agents, a man with an exceptional grasp of English. He caught me unawares, "Hello Mr Nicholson, you're the radio officer?"

"Yes," I replied.

He then proceeded to ask me if I had ever been in Korea before, and in my innocence I blurted out, "Yes, I was here in the army," before I could check myself. That, of course, was the wrong thing to say, and I was a marked man for the rest of my stay.

I was questioned daily (unofficially of course) by the ship's agent and sundry other characters who suddenly seemed to take an unhealthy interest in my previous experience of Korea. They wanted to know everything from troop movements to information about specific units. I decided to say very little, 'name, rank and number' as the phrase has it. They had, after all, been the enemy once upon a time, and you got the impression that everything you did say would be logged for future reference. The agent did seem to be happy enough though when he realised that I had served after most of the fighting was over.

We were expected to go ashore to the canteen for our evening meals, where we were surrounded by sailors from other communist countries; Russians, Bulgarians etc. The captain of each ship, including our own, was required to read a prepared statement each night praising the communist government and decrying the decadence of the west.

This nightly charade always took place before a morsel of food was served which only added to our disgruntlement, and although we were essentially allowed to prepare our own statement, the Koreans always gave us pretty clear hints about what to say. Most of the other nationalities ladled it on thick about how the 'imperialist forces had been vanquished in Korea, and how they should never have been there in the first place.' Maybe they had a point!

It soon became too much for our captain who had had a belly full of their treatment. He came to me one day, "Marconi", he said, using his nickname for me, "would you mind reading out my statement tonight? I've had enough of this repeat, repeat, repeat…"

"No bother," I said. "I'll do that for you."

When it came to my turn, the Koreans wanted to know where the captain was, and I informed them that he wasn't feeling well and was confined to his bunk. They immediately sent two soldiers to the ship, and they found the captain drinking and playing cards, and were not impressed to say the least, calling me a liar amongst other things. I still have a handwritten copy of the speech I was forced to make that night.

They put a lot of communist propaganda leaflets and books aboard, probably in the hope that it would influence some of us. Fat chance, we were sick of their ideals and constant pronouncements. We couldn't wait to get out of the place. I'd often wait until I could see one of the Koreans coming up the gangplank, and then I would grab one of their books and pretend to question other members of the crew on communist doctrine. I'm not sure if the Koreans bought it or not.

reading a statement on behalf of the captain in North Korea

We were taken to a nursery school (the best nursery school of course), which had a sixty-foot high bronze statue of Kim Il-Sung. As impressive as that was, what really stuck in the mind was the children playing with toy tanks that had 'Kill Americans' written on the side of them. What hope was there for these children?

That was three of the strangest weeks of my life, and our stay could have been longer had we not cooperated. If you weren't willing to play the game, they just ignored you and made sure that nothing happened on your ship. No cargoes landed, no cargoes loaded, no provisions and so on. They had us over a barrel, and for the sake of an early departure we were more than willing participants in their masquerade.

Singapore was a world of a difference, and another location that I enjoyed very much. It was remarkably clean and tidy, and we could certainly learn a lot from their attitude towards litter. If you dropped a cigarette butt and refused to lift it, you could expect to be fined 500 Singapore dollars at that time. I'm not sure what that would be worth now, but I seem to remember that it would have put a significant dent in your wage packet.

I even visited the famous 'Raffles' hotel, but I didn't have enough money at the time to go in and have a 'Singapore Sling.' Our accommodation ashore was slightly more down market, the Fishermen's Mission, where our entertainment consisted of watching a snake and mongoose fight accompanied by a fellow playing an instrument that looked and sounded something like a practise chanter. It is amazing what you will find to amuse yourself when needs must.

In India once, where alcohol was often taboo, we found this wee nipper of a child carrying an animal bladder that was full of grog. I don't know to this day what the hell it was, but we paid him and drank the contents without complaint. It was certainly strong and it hit the mark!

I sailed for approximately six years on British ships and approximately six years under a flag of convenience, which means that the nationality of the owner is different from the ship's country of registration. British ships were always pretty straightforward and well regulated, with a good smattering of boys from the Islands and the Western Seaboard. The same could never be said of vessels sailing under a flag of convenience. Open registry ships, as they are also known, are basically a tax dodge, and the owners of these boats were never too bothered about enforcing safety standards, minimum social standards or trade union rights for seafarers, so it made for an interesting life. These ships could be sailing under all kinds of flags, Panamanian etc, regardless of the ship's nationality. There seemed to be an almost unofficial pecking order to the whole thing. The Greeks (although many of their shipping magnates were fantastically wealthy) would buy

British merchant vessels when they were considered to be 'done', and when the Greeks were finished with them, the Chinese would be next to buy them. It must have been incredibly dodgy sailing on Chinese merchant vessels.

There were many reasons for sailing under a flag of convenience, most of them financial and, to be fair, I went after the money, which would have been fine if I had looked after the money! I should have done just that, as I was always paid very well, but the flip side was that conditions were atrocious. It certainly wouldn't be my choice today to join a vessel where you had to clean and paint your own cabin just to make it habitable. Cockroaches were rife for a start. I would often use an old jelly jar lined with oil or something similar to trap these infernal creatures. You could be sure of emptying a half jar of them every morning. I can remember coming back to the ship one night with a terrible whisky hunger on me. When I switched the galley light on to search for food, the sight of hundreds of cockroaches scurrying for safety met me. It's no wonder I got jaundice three times. Yes, conditions on British ships were much better (but the pay wasn't so good).

You would often find yourself the only British seaman onboard, especially on the Greek ships. This meant that I wasn't able to communicate even in my second language, English. I learned a bit of Greek though, and managed to get by. I found the Greeks a very sociable race; they were big into their 'raki' and 'ouzo', and there was always wine on the table at meals times, though no one ever got drunk. This was quite a departure from British ships where drinking was not officially condoned and became an underground activity. The Greeks could drink a lot, but they were always sensible with their drinking. They always had food with the alcohol; big plates of meat and so on. You might call it blotting paper, but it worked, and they didn't seem to have the same hang-ups or problems with drink as we did.

They followed a fairly healthy diet, and ate quite well onboard. A lot of black and green olives, and they always cooked with olive oil. It took me a wee while to get used to, but I enjoyed it in the end. Of course, it depended on the ship, every galley and cook were different, but they had some nice cooking, and I'm sure it didn't do me any harm.

We once caught a Hammerhead shark off the African coast. Needless to say, it was an old tramp of a boat, and we had been broken down for two or three days. The crew had put out a line (a half inch wire) with a big hunk of meat on a meat hook, in an attempt to catch something big and stave off boredom at the same time.

They did rather better than they expected and caught a fifteen to twenty foot Hammerhead shark, which they hauled aboard amid great excitement. It was cleaned, gutted and cooked within no time at all. I don't remember it being the best fish I ever ate, but it wasn't bad, and I suppose that eating a shark is better than being eaten by a shark.

There had been a terrible sand storm at the time coming off the Sahara, which left a cloud of yellow dust everywhere. You couldn't escape it. Everything was covered in it. I've never seen anything quite like it. It was very hard to fathom how people could live under conditions like that, where life is just a constant battle with nature.

The Greeks were very able seamen and were, in many ways, the equal of their British counterparts, with one notable difference. Their dress was, to say the least, a tad casual. Uniform (and a clean one at that) is a must on all British merchant vessels. This was not the case on Greek ships.

They were certainly very family orientated, the Greeks, their children were everything to them, and I also found them to be a God fearing people. They looked after their own but, by the same token, they would never have seen me in a tight spot, and for that I am grateful.

After that, I joined yet another Greek boat called 'Navmachos'. The Greeks were major players in merchant shipping. More or less everyone that I knew had sailed under a Greek flag at one time or another, and I was to join another Greek ship after that, the Protoapostolos, in September 1971. There was no shortage of work. You could basically pick and choose your jobs.

A Boat Called the Grimsay Isle

The Grimsay Isle coming into Ceallan harbour

On the 9th of January 1973 I joined a boat called the 'Efploia', and I did about three months there. Around that time though, I decided I needed to take my life in a different direction. I had grown tired of the merchant navy, having visited every conceivable part of the globe on numerous occasions. It was becoming the case that when you'd seen one bar room, you'd seen them all. It no longer held the same fascination for me, and I decided that it was time that I had something tangible to show for my years of work.

As I recall, I think my father was trying to help me, although we were often at loggerheads. He was keen for me to settle down, and would do what he could to see me settled in Uist, if indeed that was where I wanted to settle. He thought it was a good idea to have a boat, but he also thought that maybe I should be looking for a wee croft as well, like Ranish, or where Major Campbell was in Benbecula. I have to say that I could see the sense in that too.

The fishing was good at the time, and so I decided that what I needed, and wanted, was my own fishing boat, so I applied to the Highlands and Islands Development Board in Inverness for a grant and loan, to help me get started on my new venture. They were very, very helpful, and in particular Cliff Parr, whom I dealt with mostly through correspondence, and I am eternally grateful that they approved my application.

The boat was built in Wick, by James McCaughey, who came originally from the island of Stroma. I had to put down £600 before the keel was laid, and I considered that a sound investment, as he was an excellent boat builder, and still is. She measured twenty-nine feet by twelve, and was fitted with a small Lister 44·25 BPH engine, the ·25 being very important. The boat was finished in 1973, and I called her, quite fittingly I'm sure you'll agree, the 'Grimsay Isle'.

I was a very proud man when I signed off my last ship in the Persian Gulf in April 1973. I flew to London via Beirut and Greece, and made my way, as quickly as I could, to Wick, to collect my new boat. Once more, I felt very important.

It took me a while to get home. I believe it was seventy-two nautical miles to Inverness, and I had a chap onboard who gave me a hand as far as there. He was actually supposed to give me a hand through the Caledonian Canal as far as Fort William, but I think we maybe fell out, and that was the end of that.

I took the boat through the canal myself, which was quite a job, as there are thirty-two locks, which are tough to negotiate on your own. Most of the Lock Keepers were very helpful, although there were many things that they didn't need to bother doing, so you had to show them the colour of your money first of all. You're really supposed to have two men at each lock, one with the rope forward, and one with the rope aft. This nearly led to disaster at one of the locks, as the water

100

was draining out too quickly, which would have left the boat high and dry, had I not cut the ropes.

I eventually reached the Corpach basin at the end of the canal, and gave myself a good rest, which I knew I would need before the next stage of the journey. One morning I was awoken by a big rattle on the wheelhouse door, and looked up to see a big policeman in full uniform on the deck. I was pretty sure I hadn't done anything wrong, or been up to any tricks the night before, but I thought I'd better go and see what he wanted anyway.

He greeted me warmly and seemed to know me saying, "Hello Ewen, it's nice to see you." I was kind of stunned until I realised that I knew him fine, Angus MacDonald from North Uist, or Aonghas na Carnaich, as we knew him better. He just wanted to wish me all the best and a safe onward journey, which was very kind of him.

Then it was off to Tobermory in Mull where the famous accordionist and proprietor of the Mishnish Hotel, Bobby MacLeod, came onboard for a look at the new vessel. He knew me through one of my sisters who worked in the Highlander's Institute in Glasgow. He had seen the name of the boat and wondered if there was any connection with the Nicholson family, and I have to say that I felt quite honoured.

I also had cousins in Dervaig, and was keen to visit them while on the island. They were Stewarts, and Nellie Stewart ran the post office and shop in the village. Her mother was still alive at the time, and they really couldn't do enough for me. In some houses you would only get a cup of tea, but with them you were invited to a table and had a full meal. They also gave me a huge box of groceries for going home, because they felt it was a long way to Uist.

Poor Nellie is still there yet, and I'm sure she'll laugh if she ever reads this, but she was engaged to a fellow for forty-five years, and the poor man gave up and died before they could ever do anything more about it. That's often the way in the Highlands. Nobody is ever supposed to know about these relationships, but of course everyone does. Night visiting, or Caireas na h-Oichdhe as we call it in Gaelic.

There was a bit of bad weather, so I probably stayed on Mull for a day and a half, before setting off early, about three in the morning. Then the fog came, which caused me to panic a bit, as I hadn't done a big solo journey like this in my life. Yes, I had been a radio operator on countless worldwide voyages, but I hadn't been alone. And even at home, although on my own in a boat, I had only really been 'rock scratching', or sticking close to the coastline.

Eventually I was able to identify where I was and got to round about the Isle of Muck. I think I was going for the outside of Muck, but then I noticed that the boat wasn't pumping too well, which caused another panic attack.

I made for the Isle of Rhum, where I knew that the Red Deer Commission had an almost identical boat. I hoped that they would be able to help, and they were. I managed to get a hold of one of the guys from the commission, and he explained that it was very simple, I would just have to clean the seaweed out of the filter.

I was very grateful to them, although in those days they definitely didn't want you hanging around on the island for too long, which was a pity, as the weather was getting decidedly ropey. I felt that under the circumstances my best bet would be to head for Canna, where there was good shelter.

My navigational skills were fairly basic. I had the echo sounder, and I knew the speed of the boat, so I could measure speed and distance, while making allowances for tides and other variables. I was no good with the stars though. Long ago there was a family of MacLeans from Grimsay, and the man of the house used to take his own boat, which would have been a thirty-foot open craft, from Grimsay to Port Glasgow, just for groceries. He would sometimes even call in at Larne, in Ireland, for eggs. I think he must have navigated wholly on intuition, as he hardly bothered with a compass. That to me was incredible navigation.

In Canna, I made sure that I inscribed the name and number of the 'Grimsay Isle' on the rock above the harbour, where many other skippers had done so before. I'm sure it's there yet. I went to the house of big Hector MacKinnon, who was incredibly kind, and gave me a meal to keep my spirits up, until the weather improved.

I had another thirty-two nautical miles to go after that, but I had most certainly broken the back of the journey. I managed that, no bother, and was pleased to see Ceallan harbour when I eventually arrived.

The lobster fishing started in June 1973. There was quite a market for them at that time, and I knew that if I worked hard, and luck was on my side, I would soon turn a tidy profit. I had a man called Roddy MacKinnon working alongside me, and I was grateful for his expertise, which he had been honing since he was a child, and I made sure that he got a good share of the business.

We fished around the Monach Isles, which were rich lobster grounds at that time, and stayed in the old school house. The school is being renovated now, but it was pretty basic back then. It was interesting though, as the Monachs were deserted by then, although all the signs of habitation were still there. There are five main islands in the Monachs, Ceann Ear, Ceann Iar, Hearnish, Stockay and Shillay, where the lighthouse is.

It's a very impressive building, which I believe was taken out of service some time around the end of the second war. It must have been very difficult to build, and somebody was telling me, whether it's true or not, that they managed to get the bricks so high by horse power. They had a horse walking around the base of the lighthouse with a sling on, and the sling was attached to a pulley system, which hoisted the bricks up to the level where they were needed. It was the scene of a terrible tragedy, when, in the middle 30s, two lighthouse keepers were drowned, while coming across to pick up mails. The people on Ceann Iar would put up a sign on a pillar-box that the lighthouse keepers could see through their binoculars, if there was any mail for them. They came across on a Sunday evening, and met with terrible hailstones, strong winds and huge waves, which swamped their boat.

I can remember Peter Morrison, from Grimsay, taking his family to live there in the mid 40s, as the islands were still used for summer grazing. They must have stayed for three or four years, but it was hard going.

It was an amazing place, which, although deserted, seemed to grow on you. I know a fellow Angus MacDonald, from North Uist, who was born on the Monach Islands, and he said that even walking alone, you had a feeling that you maybe weren't entirely on your own. I knew what he meant. There was definitely a sense of those who had gone before, some sort of Celtic intuition.

We made our own creels under Roddy MacKinnon's direction, as he was a bit of an expert, and I was able to copy him fairly well. First of all you got larch or cane rails, which were roughly two inch by one inch. Sometimes we were given hazel rails, although our preferred material was cane, from the Philippines. Then you made a base out of larch, leaving space for one or two lumps of concrete to weight them. Some people used flat stones, as there was a plentiful supply on the Monachs. These were then covered with netting, and we waited a few days until the creels had had a good soaking before we started fishing them.

I fished lobsters in Uist for nearly ten years, although in the winter of 1974 I decided to go deep sea again for a trip. I signed on the Greek vessel 'Mparmpachristos' for a couple of months, my thinking being that it was wintertime and I wasn't really doing much fishing anyway. If I had stayed at home, I'd only have ended up in the pub anyway, and things were lean enough as they were.

By March 1975 I was back at the lobster fishing and into a season which usually lasted until October. Outwith the season, you were busy making more gear because it was unusual for you to go through a whole season without losing or damaging any. You also fished during the close season for herring, which you used as bait when the season started again and, if unsuccessful, you just phoned the MacLeans in Mallaig, and they would come to Lochboisdale or Lochmaddy and sell you a load.

We salted the herring in barrels that were made out of forty-gallon drums. You had to make sure that you had proper plastic sheeting on the top though, because if the air got in, that was the end of the bait. We salted them with coarse salt, and a small bag of salt would just about do two boxes of herring. We sometimes used mackerel as well, and we had people in Lochcarnon who were very good at salting them. That kept us going as far as bait was concerned, and ensured that we had a plentiful supply for our creels.

Roddy and I had about seven or eight-dozen creels, which suited us fine for our purposes. It was a lot of work, but we always had a good craic in the schoolhouse with the other lobstermen, when the day was done. We would commandeer some rum, and tell stories and rubbish, and I had my old accordion if the stories ran dry.

I was combining all this with my work on the family croft. My father, who was about sixty at the time, would have expected nothing else. He came out to the Monachs with me for a week, although I argued with the poor soul an awful lot.

I had an awful job one day trying to find my creels in heavy fog, about seven or eight miles out. I had no GPS or anything like that, so what I usually did was take bearings of mountains on Harris or the water tank on Benbecula, but, of course, when you don't see them, it's not a possibility. I knew that if I left the Monachs on a certain line I would find them, but sometimes it just took ages. This wasn't good enough for my Father, "You stupid fool, you should know your job by now." That was never going to help my humour. It was very frustrating, and it took me two and a quarter hours to find them, and by the time I did, the poor old man was bored and had gone below for a kip.

My drinking by this stage had progressed well beyond the social stage. I drank for thirty-eight years, and I would say that only eight of those were social. The rest were problematic for me and anyone connected with me.

It was difficult for me. Roddy MacKinnon got his own boat and left, and I had to take anyone aboard that I could. Some of them were good; some of them weren't so good. There was one guy in particular, nicknamed the Gorilla. He had a heart of gold. I remember one day the hauler wasn't working, and we had to start hauling the creels by hand. The Gorilla was immensely strong, but these were five-foot creels, and they were in ten fathoms of water. That didn't faze the Gorilla at all, and he managed to get the whole fleet of creels in. There was a bit of a swell, so we were using the motion to help us, but even so, it was an incredible achievement. I remember him saying, "Well Ewen, I can do the impossible, miracles take a bit longer."

He had a great sense of humour and would do anything for you if you kept him clear of drink, just like most of us I suppose.

I was with him at a dance in Balivanich Gym one night, when it soon became apparent that there was no taxi available to get us home. "Leave it to me boys," he says, "I'll soon get you a taxi." He was as good as his word. He stole the police car, and drove us all home in style.

Unfortunately, he got nabbed for that, and was given two months in Porterfield Prison, although he got out after a couple of weeks for good behaviour. While he was there though, there was an old jailer who took a dislike to the Gorilla, because he felt that people in prison should look miserable, and shouldn't go around with a smile on their face. The day before he got out he said to the old jailer, "See you, I'm away tomorrow. You'll be here for years yet."

There was another guy, Peter Haggerty, who sailed with me for a while too. He had an old thatched house near the south causeway. He was quite a laugh. He would tell you so many tall stories that you would start to believe that they were true. He was originally from Barra, and had been deep sea for many years himself.

The market was good at the time, and they would fly lobsters by plane from Balivanich to Glasgow or London, which meant that they were arriving on dinner tables in pristine condition. Lobsters were plentiful at that time but, of course, it didn't last. People had to get bigger boats and more creels, and the whole thing went downhill from there. I enjoyed the work though, because there was an element of excitement. Every creel that you hauled up, you were wondering what you were going to find, and it certainly kept you fit and healthy.

I found it a struggle keeping the boat going though, and unfortunately there were to be rough waters ahead in more ways than one. My father died at the age of 79 in 1980, and a few months after that, my boat sank off the Monach Isles. Both hit me pretty hard.

I was in the habit of always leaving my boat moored where it would always be floating. On that particular evening I was quite tired, and was pulling the mooring rope, and attaching it to the bow of the boat, when it fell out of my hands and went straight to the bottom. So I thought I would just move her into the shore where the sand seemed quite level. When the tide moved, she came down on her starboard, where the hauler pipes are, and unfortunately there happened to be a wee stone under her.

About six in the morning, one of my mates in the schoolhouse told me that my boat was under, which I couldn't believe. I thought he was joking, but I soon found out that he wasn't when I met religious books, cartons of milk and oilskins that had been onboard on the shore.

What a mess. It really was awful, absolutely heartbreaking. One of the religious books was entitled, 'Is This All the Life There Is?', which I have preserved to this day. I managed to bail her when the tide went out, although I nearly lost her because the tide started coming back in, and with about half an inch to spare, I managed to talk some of the other fishermen into giving me a tow home to Grimsay.

I was about four or five months waiting on the insurance company, and waiting to have her towed to Stornoway. Maybe they lost interest when they found out that I was drinking so much. That was the impression I got anyway. There was a chap there, Andy Miller-Mundy, from Harris, who was supposed to be coming to tow me with a boat called the 'Golden Chance', but I think he lost his boat around the same time on St Kilda. That was the 'chance' gone.

Eventually, a boat from Scalpay came and towed me to Stornoway, and my friend, Michael Brannigan (who was proud of telling me that he was related to Ernest Shackleton) accompanied me onboard.

We eventually got to Stornoway and booked into the Fisherman's Mission. I remember the man in charge there had a plastic hand, and he collared me coming into the building with drink, which you weren't supposed to do. He took my half bottle off me, and told me that I would get it back when I left for Uist.

The boat builders who repaired the Grimsay Isle were very lackadaisical about the whole job. They were based on Goat Island, which was well named. When I returned to Stornoway, after a number of weeks, the boat was a mess. There were no fenders, the engine was still in bits all over the boat, and I had to chase them up to get anything done. Michael Brannigan's father, Denis, who had been the vet in Uist, was very good at helping write letters to the insurance company. He could also see that I had a drink problem, but obviously thought I was still worth helping, and I will always be grateful for that.

Slowly but surely, things were pieced together, and Michael Brannigan and I sailed back to Grimsay with the refurbished boat. We had nothing but problems on our journey south. We very nearly even had a gas explosion. The boatyard had forgotten to put a copper pipe at the back of the cooker. We were heating a pie, when we started to get an awful smell of burning rubber. On top of that, the stern gland was leaking, and the rudder was in a bad way. It was dreadful.

Anyway, after another few months, and with the help of Denis Brannigan, who wrote once more to the insurance company, the boat was authorised to go to Mallaig for further repairs.

Another satisfied customer on board the Grimsay Isle.

109

Setting Course for Mallaig

I decided to take one of my drinking pals, Tommy Fraser, with me. I had offers from all kinds of people to help me take the boat to Mallaig, but they all let me down, apart from Tommy. It makes me almost cry when I think about it, but Tommy hitchhiked fifteen miles, and he was ready there in Grimsay at six in the morning to head to Mallaig.

It took us a while as the boat was only doing about four or five knots, so, when we arrived in Mallaig, there was nothing for it but to head straight for the Marine Bar. Poor Tommy was quite a character. He had a glass eye, which was the result of a car accident. One of his favourite pranks was to the leave the glass eye beside his pint glass while he nipped to the toilet. He would tell people that this was to make sure no one drunk his pint while he was away.

The Marine Bar was nearly the end of a cousin of mine, Willie Stewart, who had also been out fishing on the Monachs, although I think he was gone by the time I arrived. Anyway, Willie liked going to Mallaig and once, while on a visit, he left his mate, Hughie MacKinnon, onboard to look after his boat during a particularly high tide. After a couple of drams, the ideas were getting bigger, and Willie decided that Mallaig wasn't enough for him, he was off to the Uist and Barra dance in Glasgow. Poor Hughie was left to face the consequences when the tide went out and the boat was almost left on the pier.

Henderson's got the boat ship shape again, but by that stage I had been left in a hell of a mess financially, just about bankrupt. I still had an overdraft of about £4000, which I guess was the rough value of the boat, but I had missed out on a lot of fishing time. I had put so much into the boat that I didn't want to quit though, and I decided to give it another shot, this time not in Uist, but in Mallaig.

I decided to stay as I had really taken to the place, and it gave me the opportunity of a fresh start. I managed to get a hold of five hundred creels, and began to make good money, although most of that went over the bar counter when I was drinking, and that was the one drawback about Mallaig. There were four different pubs.

When I phoned my mother to tell her that I was staying, she told me it was the best news she had ever heard in her life. I suppose the poor woman was at her wits end with me, and a few years prior to that, she and my father had had to throw me out of the house because of my behaviour with drink. I lived in a caravan near the house, which was sad, and when I was sober, I could see that there was a problem, and that the problem was me.

My sister, who was a Jehovah's Witness, had given me an old tin shack of a house to live in, which was slightly better than a caravan. Had I had any money, or, more importantly, any sense, I could have built myself a house, or got a crofting grant to take my sister's house up to a tolerable level, but unfortunately, sense was never in it.

Looking back though, I'm glad I came to Mallaig, although I was drinking extremely heavily when I first arrived. I was also spouting religion at people while I was still drinking, and of course the two just don't go. People thought I was a hypocrite. You can't really expect to preach to people if they see you drunk the night before.

But, in many ways, coming to Mallaig was probably the making of me. I carried on drinking a lot, but I knew that things had to change. The poor staff in the Bank of Scotland could never believe it when I would come in time after time looking to withdraw more money, "Good God, are you in again after more money?" And, of course, my attitude was that it was my money, and I could do with it whatever I wanted. I had a thousand pounds in an account, and the only respect I had for myself was that I decided if I left that alone, at least it would be enough for a decent burial. It was what I called my 'coffin money'.

I would say that was the turning point in my life though. Everything seemed to be doom and gloom at home, and even though I had proved myself a very good worker, my urge to drink was becoming all embracing.

If I had the funds, I thought nothing of drinking for two or three nights, nonstop. I would be going partying, by my way of it, taking taxis all over the place, and making a general nuisance of myself. I always made for houses where I knew there was a drinker, either man or woman, it didn't matter, as long as I had a drinking pal. It was never how much I drank in the pub; it was always the carryout that caused the bother. It meant that you woke up drunk, ready for more.

A typical carryout would be a bottle of whisky, if I had money, and maybe half a dozen cans of beer. And if that ran out, you just phoned for more.

As I said earlier, I had basically fallen out with my family in Uist, and it can get pretty lonely when you're living so close to the ones you love, and who you know love you, and you are not communicating. Mallaig was different. My attitude tended to be that even if I fell out with one or two, there were plenty more people to get on with. Invariably that happened. People seemed to tolerate me with a certain amount of drink inside me. Although increasingly, I would see people doing a body swerve, out of the corner of my eye, if they saw me drinking on my own. I thought I was the centre of the universe, but I was very much mistaken.

You don't look after yourself when you're drinking either. You don't wash, you don't clean your clothes and you don't eat properly either. I was living rough on the boat for a year and nine months, which all adds up to a pretty miserable life. It was pretty hard going. My only central heating was a bottle of banana rum. It was no life at all really, and as you know, boats and alcohol just don't mix. I was pulled out of the harbour on at least four occasions, which is really amazing, because other guys weren't so lucky once.

There is always help for people with any kind of addiction, be it drug or drink related or gambling. The difficult bit is being able to admit that you have a problem. Once you admit to yourself and others, you can face it fair and square, and you'll start to win the battle. That's the way I found it anyway.

Eventually I ended up with £5 in the bank and a load of debts. So, reluctantly, I put the boat up for sale, and placed an advert in the fishing news. The next step for me was to be placed into the care of Dunain House where I would hopefully dry out and kick the bottle for good.

Dunain House was a part of Craig Dunain Mental Hospital, in Inverness. When I arrived, I was taken to see a consultant, who asked me if I had ever been there before. I told him that yes I had, and that, in fact, I had been born there, which meant he thought I was really off my head.

Actually, I was telling the truth, as he found out later. My mother had been quite ill during her pregnancy with me and, at that time, Craig Dunain was the only place that dealt with pre or post-natal conditions. So my mother was taken there and that's where I was born.

I was virtually penniless at the time but, even so, I only went to Inverness semi-voluntarily. A certain gentleman from Mallaig was kind enough to give me a lift there, and I don't suppose he ever experienced such bullshit in all his life. The alcohol was wearing off, and I was beginning to regret going to a place like that. I even demanded a quarter bottle on the way there, and although he wasn't happy, the poor man got one just to shut me up.

By the time I got there, I was too drunk to get in to Dunain House. They just couldn't let me in, as I would have upset people who were well into their rehabilitation. I had no option but to go to the Beechwood, Church of Scotland hostel.

They would only take you in if you were drunk. It was a sort of staging post for the 'big house,' as it were.

The next morning there was a nurse from Gairloch at my bedside, and she gave me quite a laugh. "You were proposing marriage to me last night," she said. Who would have a drunk like me!

Dunain House was a different story all together. It was a serious wake up call. For the first time, I came into contact with people who were in the same boat, and were often much worse. Some had inflicted irreversible brain damage on themselves because of their drinking, and if that didn't bring me to my senses, nothing would have. I saw many people wandering round the grounds, who had ended up with what they call a 'wet brain' because of their drinking. Their minds had gone completely and they were no longer able to function like you or I. It really brought me to my senses. I said to myself, "Well Ewen, you don't want that as your fate."

I am glad to say that that wasn't my fate. God had other plans for me, and for that I am eternally grateful. There is one regret however. Maybe if I had been a more sober chap, I would have had a wife and family, and that would have been wonderful, especially given my love for children. But it was not in the great plan. I do feel though, that maybe you haven't achieved an awful lot if you are not married. It is perhaps just a status symbol, but I think family life is something I would have enjoyed.

I listened very closely to the speakers who came to see us as part of the drying out programme. They encouraged us to go to as many AA meetings as possible, because you could identify with people there, and there was strength and support in numbers. It made a change for me to listen, because when I was drinking, I was always the talker, nonstop, but in the AAs, they say, 'take the cotton wool out of your ears and stick it in your mouth.'

Drinking was an endemic part of my life at that time, and I don't suppose my domestic situation helped. My poor neighbour at the time, Cath MacLennan, was my boozing buddy as often as not, and she was actually taken to Craig Dunain a week before me. In fact, on the night she was taken away, I, half jokingly, said to her that she'd better reserve a bed for me. Little did I know that, within a week, my joke would become reality.

The first morning that I went in poor Cathy looked at me with horror because I still had on my fishing gear; the smelly boots, and the 'Compo' hat. She said, "God Ewen, you should have cleaned yourself before you came to visit me." I said, "You've got it wrong Cathy, I'm an inmate the same as yourself."

She was sober by this stage. She'd been in a week, and had cleaned up, but was still convinced that I had come to visit her.

While inside, there is absolutely no possibility of gaining access to booze, and they know every trick in the book when it comes to sneaking it in. They do, after all, deal with some pretty determined customers. Doctors come round every so often, and they are interspersed with social workers. The regime is pretty tight, and you have to have permission to do anything. I was there for about a week and a half before they deemed me fit even to have a walk in the grounds. If they say that you are not getting out; you are not getting out. It's always in the back of their minds that you might jump on a bus and head straight for the bright lights of Inverness, and, in all honesty, it's always in the back of your mind too.

When I was allowed out, the first thing I did was to get lost in the trees, and the man that let me out informed me that the next time I went for a walk, he would have a ball of wool ready at his desk.

There is no miracle cure for alcoholism, but going to Dunain House was the best thing I ever did in my life. It was the first step on the ladder to sobriety, and I have been over twelve years sober now, although I am still working on my quality of sobriety. You are encouraged to get rid of resentment. You don't let people who have wronged you occupy a space in your head. If you do, you're the one with the problem.

I went to several meetings at Dunain House, which I found very helpful. There would be thirty or forty other people there, and they had all been through the wringer too, which helps, as you no longer feel alone. Also, you can't kid on another alcoholic.

The downside is that many alcoholics just hit the skids again as soon as they are cleaned up. There may be many reasons for that. I have to say that I felt very safe in Dunain House, and I really didn't want to go back to Mallaig at all, as I associated that with my drinking. I was horrified by the thought. I'd really lost my nerve, so I can understand why people fall off the wagon so soon.

I had to go back though. My home was in Mallaig, as was my boat, although she was still up for sale, and I'm sure I would have drunk any money that I made out of that too. Alcoholics are desperate people, and I feel sorry for those that have to live with them. I have lived alone for many years, and now I can understand why. Why should an alcoholic make somebody else's life a misery? I think it's totally disgusting now, but when I was drinking I couldn't see that. When you're drunk, you think that everyone else is drunk, and of course they're not.

As I said earlier, I should have been in for longer, but they were closing the unit before the new one opened. Dunain House is no more, but it certainly had its fair share of Highland people through the door, especially from the islands.

I don't really keep in touch with anyone that I was there with, although I still see people at meetings. We have a sort of unofficial network of support. For instance, a man approached me in Fort William the other day and asked me how I was. I asked him if he knew me, and he said no, not really, but he had seen me at AA meetings. It was nice of him to come and make himself known. We shook hands, and I asked him how long he had been sober. He said he had been sober for thirty years, which made him happy, although he tempered that by saying, "I'm sober today, and I don't know about tomorrow." That really sums it up. We take each day at a time. You are always an alcoholic.

I knew that I had a problem with drink very early on in my merchant navy days, but I was young, and had a strong constitution, so it never interfered with my work. I could get over binges quite easily. Now, when I say a binge, the longest I ever had was about three weeks, and that was drinking solidly, everyday. Not gulping it, but it was there all the time.

The money I must have spent would be frightening too. Having said that, heavy drinkers, who are maybe not alcoholics, probably spent just as much, if not more, because they were drinking everyday. It probably did them as much physical damage, although the mental scars will not be there.

It was very rare, in fact, that I would be physically sick with a hangover but, my word, the mental anguish was torture. I suffered terrible depression, and people would say, "Why do you take a drink the next day?" The answer was perfectly simple, because I was scared of what I would go through if I didn't have one. I suffered hallucinations, and could often hear voices. Things like my aunty sitting on top of the wardrobe, giving me hell, and she'd been dead for years. There was even three days once that I couldn't put the lights off. I was that scared. It all seemed so real to me.

People would often see the happy go lucky figure in the pub, and they didn't think it was doing me any harm. But little did they know the full extent of the harm it was doing me, and what I would be suffering.

I used to go back to the pub the following day, and all my darkest thoughts would start preying on me. I would wonder if I had been barred the night before. Then the paranoia would kick in, and I would think, my God, they're taking an awful long time to serve me. They were just serving other people, but I wouldn't see that.

I could never remember what I had done when I was drinking. I used to suffer the most terrible memory blanks. I would get into fights and terrible arguments with people, and then couldn't recall a thing, and I would walk for miles, not knowing where I was or what I was doing there. I remember coming from a dance in Benbecula during the late 50s. They were just starting to build the bridge at the time, and two engineers found me and helped me into my father's boat. I must have got home, but I can't remember a thing about going through that maze of islands. People tell me that that is impossible, but I know it isn't, and I'm certainly not proud of that.

My tipple was always rum or whisky. I never graduated onto the likes of meths or brasso, although I'm not saying that wouldn't have happened. I was just lucky that I got a grip in time. Occasionally I took wine, which was a habit I had started at home in Uist. Creagorry Hotel was in the Guiness Book of Records because of the amount of carryouts they used to sell and, as a sideline of that, the owners sold fairly potent cheap wine, which soon became known as electric soup. It was a favourite trick of the heavy drinkers to slope off to the toilet and 'glug, glug' at a bottle of the cheap wine, before getting stuck into the beer and whisky.

Myself and poor Tommy Fraser would always be skint by Sunday, and the owner, Domhnall Ruadh, used to give us a sub. He would then write out on an ordinary bit of paper, a note, which read something like 'promise to pay the bearer on demand.' Of course, when I sobered up, I would have a pile of these, and I wouldn't have a clue what they meant.

It's hard to know where this disease stems from. Maybe it's genetic, or maybe it's a confidence thing. I know plenty people who will use alcohol for 'Dutch courage.' I could never understand why big, strong Highland men had to do that. They would go to a dance, for example, and they'd be so damned shy, me included. I would have to have a drink before I would have dreamed of asking a woman up for a dance. I don't know what the hell for. I happened to be quite a good dancer, and would be doing quite well up until about halfway through the night. But then I would be going outside for more drink. I could never keep myself at that enjoyable level. At a certain stage, the balance would be tipped, and suddenly alcohol held far more attraction for me than any pretty girl in the hall. I could never understand why all these other guys would be going home with a girl at the end of the night, while I was left with nobody. Now I understand why. I learned the hard way.

Most alcoholics are in denial though. They realise they have some sort of problem, but they probably don't realise how bad. They're studying the situation from the inside, and they don't have the panoramic view afforded to everyone else. It must be pitiful when you see someone you love destroying themself. The personality changes, and soon you are no longer the same person.

My father was a drinker too, and used to get quite rowdy with a drink in him. That is to say that he was much nicer in the company of other people than he was with his own family when he was drinking. I can remember being quite scared if he came in at night with a drink on him. He would argue with my mother and that bothered me, although my brother Angus, who was stronger willed than me would just tell me to let them get on with it. I felt sorry for my mother.

I always managed to keep my drinking pretty much in check when I was deep sea. That was surprising because, apart from tankers where alcohol was restricted, there was plenty access to alcohol, and I don't just mean shore leave. As an officer of sorts, I was allowed two or three bottles of beer a week, and maybe the odd tot of rum, and if your ship had a chief steward, you slipped him a couple of quid, and a bottle would miraculously appear in your cabin. You then became very popular with your mates.

I had a mate at sea that I still keep in touch with, and we used to booze together quite a lot. He came to me one day convinced that someone was drinking his aftershave. I laughed and assured him that I had nothing to do with it. However, a couple of weeks later, he told me that he had found out who the culprit was. The second cook had been getting stuck into it. Everyone had some way of getting a drink

I knew of dockers in Liverpool who became highly adept at pilfering drink. They had an arrangement with the crews of ships carrying spirits, whereby they would make a bad job of landing one case, and would make sure that the corner bottle got broken 'accidentally', dividing the remaining bottles between themselves and the crew.

You really were surrounded by alcohol. It was a fact of life. Everyone drank, and so, what chance did you have if you developed a problem? I know I have been very lucky, and many have not been so fortunate, but I'm determined to stay lucky this time.

Sometimes, if I'm under pressure, I still feel the need for a drink, and sometimes, after being sober for twelve years, I get sneaky feelings like I would be able to handle it now. I know enough through the AAs to ignore that though. The chances of handling it now are at best 5%, and I'm certainly not going to risk it.

I could dish out drink to people now, without feeling the need to have one myself, although I still wouldn't be too keen to go and order a soft drink in a bar, as many of the old feelings are still present. I remember being at a family wedding, and one of my brothers-in-law handed me his glass of whisky when he was up dancing, and I have to say that I felt very guilty holding that glass. The fumes were still quite nice.

Mallaig was my saviour though, and I was glad I did return when I came out of Dunain House. I made sure that I went to two AA meetings a week, as it was very early days. I was also reinstated as a Jehovah's Witness. I knew that my drinking was not of a tolerable standard for the Witnesses, but they were prepared to take me back.

I also knew I had to do something to get me back on the road to profit with the boat. Even so, ordering five hundred prawn creels could have been viewed as pretty drastic, but my thinking was that prawns were so plentiful that I couldn't go wrong.

My drinking had seriously affected my business, and, of course, I wasn't always sober enough to go to sea but I worked as often as I could, hangover permitting. I even employed one or two young local boys, who proved to be dedicated workers and a good laugh as well. I was working day trips, and a maximum of a nine-hour day, which suited me fine.

Some days I just couldn't face it, although I always had an emergency stash of alcohol ready for just such an event. If I was just off the drink though, I wouldn't touch that, as I knew fine well that one was never enough, and that would be another day wasted.

I always tried to do my best though, and was a stickler for keeping proper records of the fishing. I know that if I had been sober I would have done very well and even had plans to branch out into tourism, which is something that I am enjoying immensely in my old age.

I thoroughly enjoy taking people out on day excursions, especially families and wee kids. There is nothing like seeing the smile on a child's face when they catch that first fish on a line. It is so rewarding, and puts all the bad times into perspective.

It was a man, Peter MacLean, that first suggested the possibility of excursions to me. He said, "You should get cracking and take people out on your boat," which is something I had never considered before. The more I thought about it, the more I liked the idea. I always enjoyed meeting people, I could spin a good yarn, and my knowledge of the sea was as good as anyone's.

I probably started in earnest around 1990, after I had made sure that I had all the necessary licenses and safety equipment, which was a bit of an adventure in itself. The regulations are being continually tightened all the time, and while I would agree with most of them, they are really aimed at people that have no proper knowledge of the sea. I always endeavour to keep up to date with all the latest safety developments, and sat a course last year, which would actually entitle me to skipper a bigger boat, so I felt pretty good about that (not that I'll ever need it). I also did a high-speed powerboat course, which prompted one or two funny looks from the younger guys on the course. But I did it and enjoyed it. All these things help to put your passengers' minds at rest, and that's important. It all adds to their enjoyment of a trip, if they feel safe going to sea with you.

I don't suppose it was really a case of seeing a gap in the market, or worrying about the future of fishing. I just fancied trying something different, a new challenge, and running excursions gave me that challenge. I've always liked being around people, and fishing can be quite a lonely business, even when times are good.

I'm so glad that I decided to give it a go. I've met so many wonderful and interesting people on day trips. I've had the British High Commissioner to Canada aboard, who was a very decent chap. He asked how much I charged for a day hire, and I told him that I would have to have a look at the leather in his shoes first. I've also had Lord and Lady Butler, who hired my boat to go to where Gavin Maxwell wrote his famous book, 'A

Ring of Bright Water'. I've also had three or four film crews charter the boat for the day. The only problem for them being the engine noise. One of the programmes was a documentary on Russian Klondikers that were anchored in Loch Nevis. That was very interesting, and myself and the director, Morag Stewart, who is also from Grimsay, were invited to have a meal with one of the Russian captains. They were very hospitable, and gave each of us five tins of sardines as a leaving present.

Everyone seems to enjoy it, and everyone is treated the same, although I would like to think that I am always polite and respectful. Many people send me photos along with letters thanking me for the day. I keep them all, and to date, I have an album with over two hundred and fifty photos in it, which resides in the Mallaig tourist office. Whenever anyone asks about my boat, the staff in the tourist office show them the album, and all they see is smiling faces, which usually clinches the deal. I also have a fantastic DVD of the boat, that was very kindly made for me by a botanist friend of mine. It features many wonderful photographs that he took himself, and footage

Feeding my pet seal Annabelle

123

of his own family. In fact, it is that good, that I could sit and watch and believe that I was on holiday myself.

I do all kinds of trips, and may do three sailings in one day, with each lasting a couple of hours. I am allowed a maximum of ten passengers, and that doesn't include my pet seagull Rebecca pictured below:

My pet seagull Rebecca

There is also Jimmy the cat, who has his own life jacket. I've had Jimmy for about seven years, and he's very obedient. He went missing for ten days once and I was very down. The wee children in the school were great though, they kept saying to me, "Don't worry Ewen, we'll look for Jimmy." He came back late one night. I heard this scratching sound at the door, and I opened it to find this poor bedraggled thing. Nobody believes me about the pet seagull, because there are thousands in Mallaig, but it is true. I was ashore for three months, and it

124

was the same seagull that came aboard to see me everyday, and I call her Rebecca. I also have one or two pet seals. The one I had out in Canna was called Sammy, and one of the big ones in Mallaig, who only has one eye, is called Nelson. He's a big grey seal that eats fish out of your hand. Some of the other boys in Mallaig went one better though. They have a pet otter, Scar Face, which sleeps on their boat at night, so I'm hoping to tap into that market as well.

Scarface and me

We often go ashore somewhere for people to stretch their legs and have a picnic, if the weather is favourable. I also provide a running commentary, and I enjoy having a blether with people, which helps to pass the time. There is definitely an art to making a commentary, and it is one that I am learning. I probably talk too much, and I find that if I say less, the passengers will ask more, and that seems to work better, although the art of conversation doesn't seem to be what it was.

I make sure now, as I'm getting older, that the children have a nice time. They all get a shot at the wheel of the boat, which goes down a storm. I've actually got two wheels, a big one and a small one, so nobody misses out, and if somebody is too small to reach the wheel, I just put a bucket under them like 'Oor Wullie.' I have a couple of boxes of chocolates and biscuits too, which I hand out if morale is flagging.

I have come to know a family by the name of Holmes very well through the boat. They come on holiday to this area every year from Aberdeen, and I call the father, Alan, 'Sherlock Holmes'. Their wee girl, Morna, she'll be about ten now, is very keen on the 'Grimsay Isle', in fact, the last time they were here, she enjoyed her trip so much that she refused to leave the boat. Morna is an extremely musical wee girl and can play the fiddle and dance an Irish jig.

There was a wee boy of eleven or twelve who once wrote a comment in my visitor's book. It was only a short comment, but it almost left me in tears, 'Ewen, the best day of my life!' I'll never forget that. You can't put a price on it. Wee kids like that will always remember acts of kindness as they grow older and make their way in life. I see it as trying to put something back in to a world where I upset an awful lot of people. Maybe I've found my vocation. I just wished I discovered it many years before I did.

I still fish about two hundred and fifty creels, which I enjoy for the most part, although sometimes I could see it far enough. Sometimes I feel I would rather concentrate completely on being a passenger vessel, but I suppose it is about striking a balance. I'm very lucky actually, as I have a Spanish buyer who takes the shellfish off me. He's willing to take live prawns, and his prices are good, and it's still good to be fishing when the weather is fine. I do enjoy the solitude at times as well. As I said, it's about striking a balance.

It's funny the twists that life takes as well. I had a shipping magnate by the name of Brocklebank onboard once. He lived in Grosvenor Square in London. It was funny after having been deep sea myself for twelve years, and now here I was with one of the big shots on my wee boat. He was a nice man though, and I charged him just the same as I would anyone else.

In the twenty-three or so years that I've been in Mallaig, I've always enjoyed going back to Uist, whenever I got the chance. It was a bit slow (nine and a half to ten hours), and I took some chances with the weather, but I always got there. I felt good about it, and I always felt as if I was going home. I would be greeted warmly by my family, especially when I had got a grip on my drinking.

The last time I was over was maybe about three years ago, and I took Jimmy the cat for company. Just to show him the old country. I was working on the croft with my sister, and I was scared that Jimmy would run off, so I put him on about twenty yards of twine, and he had a whale of a time playing in the rashes.

I have a wee friend from Malta, Semsi, who is also a Jehovah's Witness. She has seven cats, including her favourite, Sooty. She and her family moved back to Malta a couple of years ago, and this caused a problem, as it looked as if Sooty and the other cats would not be allowed to go. I phoned the wee soul and tried to cheer her up by telling her that my sister Effie, in Uist, would take them, as she likes cats, but Semsi was having none of it. She said, "That's fine Ewen, but you can tell Effie that she'll need to take me as well."

With my sister Ann and some of our witness friends

A Jehovah's Witness

I had been aware of the Witness movement from about 1957, because a girl I was seeing in Greenock at the time had an aunty who had joined. My sister Ann, who was in America, became a witness then in 1959 but, at the age I was then, I never really took any heed of that. I failed to see the relevance, which is a fairly natural reaction when you are young.

Ann and her husband were employed in domestic work by various different families, and met Jehovah's Witnesses through that. I think they were actually looking for some kind of meaning to life, when they encountered a couple from Brooklyn, and took to what we call 'the truth' right away. Ann told me that there was definitely a ring of certainty to the whole thing from the minute she began to listen, and she was hungry for more.

She was keen to convert others and, of course, she had a big job on her hands with me. I was interested in similar questions, like what are we doing, and why do we die young? But I was also interested in alcohol, and that took precedence. She preached to me and tried to teach me for twenty eight years, and I used to think, Jehovah God must be very short of witnesses if he's interested in the likes of me. But Ann knew better. She knew that he could read hearts. I still have hundreds of questions, but the more I study and learn about my faith, the more the questions are answered.

I have to be honest and say that I saw it, at first, as an insurance policy, a way of insuring eternal life. It certainly helped me to deal with my drinking, and in 1990 I was baptised in the High School pool in Edinburgh.

I had attended a convention at Murrayfield, along with twenty thousand others. What struck me immediately, was how organised they were, without a policeman in sight. They did their own traffic management, and everything was nice and clean and, what struck me most, was that 99% of the people had a smile on their face. I decided that I would love, someday, to be a part of that. I was still drinking though, and that would have to be sorted first.

I did move towards it though, and as I said, I was eventually baptised in 1990. I had found a contentment at last, although I still wasn't in complete control of my drinking demons. Two years after being baptised, I decided to try an experiment in controlled drinking, with disastrous consequences.

It is a commonly held belief that Jehovah's Witnesses do not drink, but this is a myth. Most Witnesses do drink, though not to excess, and certainly not as alcoholics. Jesus Christ turned the water into wine, and at the marriage feast of Cana in Galilee they ran short of wine, which suggests that there were relatives of mine in attendance.

My drinking was over the score though. Elders came and pleaded with me to change my ways. I was giving the organisation a bad name. In fact, what it amounted to was hypocrisy. If you saw me coming home drunk on Saturday night, what would be the chances of you listening to me, if I called to give you a Bible message on Sunday morning. It was crazy and people, not just Witnesses, were so disappointed in me, because I had done so well to kick the habit.

The Witnesses were left with no alternative but to revoke my fellowship, which was heartbreaking after all I had done to clean up my act. I was offered a way back, but I wasn't prepared, then, to be repentant, and it took two or three months before I was prepared to go back to the Kingdom Hall in Fort William.

Once there, I had to sit at the back, which made me feel like a skunk, and that was basically what I was. You are not included in the meeting at this stage, and they don't talk to you either. Genuine evidence of repentance is needed before you can be accepted into the fold again. An elder, always a discerning person, will come and have a word with you, bearing in mind that they have had worse than me to deal with. Anyway, after about a year of proving my repentance, I was welcomed back in, and I never intend to go back out again. If somebody offers me a better way to worship God, I'll go for it, but I haven't found one yet.

It is an amazing challenge to be a Witness. We have a loving message, but it is quite a forceful one too. This doesn't always go down well with people, but we feel that is the way our teaching needs to be.

We believe in the Day of Judgement, and we believe in the resurrection, and we also believe that most people will come back on earth again. People say, 'How is that possible?' but we say that for Jehovah God, who created the earth, it's not a big problem to put us back together again. We believe that we will actually recognise one another, and I certainly look forward to seeing my brother Archie. It's a wonderful thing to look forward to.

We are a Christian religion, and stick to the Bible and God's word rigidly. We also believe that there is a great war going on between good and evil. It is not a sect, as some would have you believe, but a fully-fledged worldwide movement, which many people may not understand. We have a huge number of practising Jehovah's Witnesses in Africa, even in some of that continent's most troubled regions. In that terrible conflict in Rwanda between Tutsi and Hutu many Witnesses on both sides sheltered fellow Witnesses regardless of ethnic background, knowing full well that in so doing they were risking their lives. People in Africa tend to embrace religions that will help their everyday lives. By following our doctrine, they will stop drinking, stop smoking and stop chewing beetle nut, and the money they save on these vices can be spent on food and improving their standard of living.

We also have a large following in Japan, somewhere in the region of 200,000, and they make very dedicated Witnesses. Italy has somewhere in the region of 242,000 as opposed to only 120,000 in the UK, which has a similar population.

I don't remember a precise moment where I suddenly decided that I wished to devote my life to this religion. As I recall it was a very gradual process. In fact, my poor sister, who had been encouraging me for well nigh twenty-eight years, was almost giving up. She used to do a bit of preaching in South Uist many years ago, and I would turn up in the middle of the night in a drunken stupor with a Bible question that I was sure she couldn't answer. That was the way of it; constant questioning, always trying to catch her out. I knew best.

Her and her poor husband would get out of bed (which says a lot), make me a cup of tea to sober me up, and give freely of their time to answer any query I may have had.

Her answers must have had some effect on me though. It was a gradual swaying as I said. A steady trickle, which grew to be a torrent. My brother in law, who passed away a couple of years ago, actually suggested that maybe I try a period of Bible study with a qualified elder or ministerial servant, which I agreed to, and that was a fair turning point in my life. We are not a particularly emotional religion. Other religions are. I used to hear people say, "At ten o'clock at night the Lord spoke to me," whereas I am pretty sure that the Lord was fed up of speaking to me. My view was that I had a lot of living to do yet before turning to religion, but I didn't have what you might call an epiphany. There were no bright lights or voices calling out to me. It was a very gentle process.

I suppose I had to hit rock bottom, and I did. Let's look at the facts. I had been pulled out of Mallaig harbour four times. I had drunk all my money away. The boat was up for sale. Very few people spoke to me any more, and those that did, did so out of pity more than anything else. I was a physical and mental wreck. I knew by the time I needed that drink first thing in the morning just to function that I had had enough.

One or two in Mallaig, who were AA members already, helped me a lot. One couple in particular took me along to my first meeting, which was a bit of a non-starter, as I had to drink a bottle of sherry first, such was my apprehension. Dutch courage they call it.

Of course, when you consider my spiritual salvation, you would have to ask, 'Why the Jehovah's Witnesses?' After all, I had been brought up in the Church of Scotland, in what was a fairly God fearing home. I know that over the twenty-eight year period I mentioned earlier, I read an awful lot of 'Witness' literature, copious amounts in fact. If the truth be told, I was always trying to find fault, but I couldn't, and eventually it began to dawn on me that maybe this was the way, and maybe I was the one at fault. I had a friend whom I used to drink with. He was a Congregational minister, and a rugby player, and my word could he drink. He didn't like Witnesses, and was always writing questions for me to take to my sister. Eventually, my sister got fed up of answering these, and she said to me, "Right, Ewen, you can start answering your friend's questions." I did, and it was really through things like that that I was saved.

At the periscope of HMS Splendour, somewhere beneath the Sound of Raasay where I had my last drink.

I consider that in many ways I have lived two lives. It is one of the first things I learned at the AA meetings. You have your life with alcohol, and you have your life without, and the two are not compatible. Even the Bible tells us that a drunkard will not inherit God's kingdom. There are not really any facets of my previous life that I miss, because it was a drunkard's life, and I was, at times, such a disgrace. I want to bury the past, but not totally, because there has to be some reminder of the man I was. It is important, as part of my ministry, that I can tell people of the life I had, to show them that there is real hope.

It is not easy. As a Witness I have encountered much difficulty and intolerance, some of it even in my own family. My own brother dislikes Witnesses, and will not hear mention of the subject. Often, I point him towards Mathew 10: 35-36, where Jesus comes to the earth. In it, we have the option to follow him or not, but if we do, we are warned that some of your own household will be your worst enemies. And in the Witnesses, we are told that, as a Christian, if you are finding things easy you are not doing your job properly.

As a Jehovah's Witness, I am expected to go round people's doors preaching the word. This is a very difficult part of our work. Most people cannot be bothered listening, although I have to say that, in the Highlands I find people, on the whole, very tolerant. Usually people are too busy, "I'm on the phone," or, "I'm changing a nappy," that kind of thing. You do get the odd person who rants and raves, but that is when your training comes to the fore. You must not allow yourself to become heated. Discuss, yes, but don't argue. Wish the person well, and always remember that they may be having a bad day, or terrible problems of their own. The last person they may want to see is a Jehovah's Witness.

It is a trial, but I have always loved a challenge. Most of it you could never do under your own strength. We receive divine help, of that I am sure. I am not brave enough to knock on all the doors in Mallaig. I certainly pick my targets, but I have nice wee conversations with people, and I am always interested to see if they got anything from the last magazine I left with them. I tell people not to take the magazines unless they are really reading them. I don't want them to take one just to please me. At the end of the day, the hardest door is the one you leave behind at the start of the day. I find it difficult to be nice if I'm receiving a hard time, but I might crack a joke, or do my best to defuse the situation.

We certainly don't 'Bible thump.' We don't believe that you will burn in hell like some churches, who would put the very fear of God into people. We believe that you should come away from a service happy and spiritually nourished, not in fear and anguish.

It is difficult though and especially so for those who have been brought up in the faith. I wasn't. I had my chance to see the bright lights before turning to the truth later in life, so I can see the problems that young Witnesses face when they reach adulthood. There are many choices to make, and many temptations, and many will leave the faith at that point. We have a saying though, 'You may leave the truth, but the truth never leaves you.'

When I started going round in Mallaig first of all, I was terrified. It was maybe part of my alcoholism, but I was worried what people would say, and what they would think about me. Would they think I had cracked up? Nowadays, I'm very open about it, and it doesn't bother me at all, and why should it?

I am just an ordinary Witness. There are five meetings a week, where I am supposed to try and take in as much as I can. We study the Bible book by book, which I have always found very interesting, and then we have open sessions of question and answer. I'm privileged in a way, I have a wee job in the book cupboard, which makes me feel quite important for the right reasons, although we are all ministers of God's word.

I would say that most people in Mallaig respect me now, and I can understand why many of them were unsure of my motives at first. I'm sure that many understand that often, to stop one thing, you have to start another, and in my case it was stopping drink and discovering the Bible.

Life's Characters

I have always taken a great delight in meeting people. This stems from my earliest days and has remained with me throughout my life. People never cease to amaze me, and I am always interested to hear someone's story.

I have been fortunate to meet some wonderful characters over the years, individuals that have left a lasting impression, for all kinds of different reasons. What follows, is just a brief selection of some of those men and women.

I would like to start this chapter by making mention of my friend Lachlan MacDonald, who was originally from St Kilda. In fact, Lachlan was one of the last surviving St Kildans and had been evacuated from the islands with the other remaining inhabitants in 1931.

Lachlan and his wife Nancy, who was originally from Benbecula, lived in Glen Nevis, where Lachlan worked with the Forestry Commission for many years. It is a strange fact that many of the St Kildans found employment with the Forestry Commission after having been born and bred on treeless islands.

I can't remember exactly how I met Lachlan but I suppose when you are one of those people who enjoys talking to anyone, you tend to forget.

Another friend, whom I remember well, was Duncan Gillies from Mallaig. Duncan was a fine piper and was for many years a member of the world famous Glasgow Police Pipe Band under Pipe Major John MacDonald (South Uist), a fact of which Duncan was rightly proud. Duncan was a great character and a wonderful storyteller, and had many tales from his youth and his days as a policeman in Glasgow.

Like all great raconteurs, Duncan would take a long time over his stories, and would inevitably finish with the rebuke

"You're not listening to me!" which was probably true, as we had more than likely heard the story many times before.

Anyway, I had an old car at the time, and I decided to take my old friend Duncan to Glen Nevis to meet Lachlan MacDonald. I had arranged the visit and, on the appointed day, we headed off. It was very interesting because Lachan would have been in his late teens or early twenties when he left St Kilda, and so his was a first hand account of what life was like at that time, and I knew that Duncan would enjoy his stories. They had never met before, but hit it off immediately, as I knew they would. It was great to get an opportunity to bring those two wonderful old gentlemen together, one of those experiences that you just can't put a price on.

Duncan Gillies and I were firm friends. Our conversation was always in Gaelic, and whoever was the soberest would make the cup of tea at the end of the night. That's the way things worked.

Duncan was originally from Loch Nevis side, where his father was a shoemaker, amongst other things, as I suppose he was a crofter / fisherman also. In fact, when Sir Cameron MacIntosh was renovating some of the old buildings there, they found leather in the ground and other evidence of shoemaking. They lived near the track which runs from Tarbert to Kyles Morar, where Duncan and his brothers and sisters attended the little school. Theirs was a way of life now all but gone, and I could see many parallels with my own upbringing on Grimsay.

As a teenager, Duncan went to work at the 'big house' in Inverie, which he himself regarded as slavery. There were nine gardeners employed on the estate at the time, and they had to scythe a huge area of grass amongst other jobs. Duncan would be placed in the middle with a man scything ahead of him and a man scything behind him, which meant that you had to keep the rhythm going no matter how tired you felt, or you could

138

end up losing your feet. Although, as he would say himself, "That tale may have had whiskers on it."

After that he came to Mallaig to work in the West Highland Hotel, or the Station Hotel as it was known then. He would have been a porter or something similar, which he considered a posh job compared to the 'slavery' in Inverie. Eventually, he made it to Glasgow where he enjoyed a long and successful career in the police.

He was held in high regard locally both as a gentleman and piper, and was always asked to adjudicate at the piping competitions at the local highland games. I always enjoyed attending these events, even though I drank too much, and can remember Duncan in full highland dress judging the pibroch and light music with a big glass of 'nectar' near at hand.

I am very grateful that I have had the chance to know people like Duncan. We should all take the time to associate with our elders, as we can learn so much from them. My father used to say, "Be kind to little children and very old people, and if you have time, be kind to the ones in between."

Duncan was an authority on the history of the Mallaig area and could remember many of the now abandoned settlements along Loch Nevis including Ardnamurach and Camusaneighinn when they supported large communities.

There have been many occasions since when Duncan's knowledge would have proved invaluable. A few years ago, I took a party of Belgians up Loch Nevis. They wanted to go to a place at the head of the loch called Finiskaig. I felt a wee bit embarrassed, as I hadn't a clue where this was, and although I asked around the pier in Mallaig, nobody seemed to know. The poor Belgians had to show me eventually on their Ordnance Survey map.

Finiskaig, as it turned out, was just near Sourlies, another place that Duncan had many stories about. Apparently there had been a poor woman that lived up on the hill near there, who had lost three brothers during the Great War. The effects of such a loss on a community of that size cannot be overstated. Sourlies had supported a large population which increased during the summer months, as the people of the area took their cattle to the sheilings to graze on the rich summer pastures, but the war ripped the heart out of that many other communities.

As a young man in the City of Glasgow Police, Duncan eventually made the rank of Sergeant in what he called himself 'the enquiries department'. He always emphasised that bit most thoroughly and banged his hands or stamped his feet to make sure you got the message.

There are not many people living on either side of Loch Nevis now. One of the last that I know of is Donald MacDonald from Tarbert. An incredible man himself, Donald is that last survivor of a family of eight or nine, and decided to get married for the first time in his nineties. I remember Donald's sister Jessie Ann also. She lived to a great age, 96 I think, maybe more. She was a lovely woman who, unfortunately, had begun to lose her mind with age. I think she used to enjoy me speaking Gaelic to her. She used to ask me whom I had seen coming over the hill to Tarbert that day, and I would tell a few white lies, which I'm sure the good Lord wouldn't have minded.

Donald is a quiet man, and it was always nice to hear him talking about his younger days, if you got him on form. They had a hard life, but a good one, and certainly knew how to enjoy a ceilidh. If we add up all the time we spend watching television, it would be better spent visiting, as the old people used to; blasting away at pipes and telling stories, many of which were made up then and there. If there were children about, there would maybe be a story about the 'Each Uisge' (Water Horse), which was a clever way of deterring children from playing on or near water.

Donald also told me a little bit about the post office that his family ran at Tarbert, and about the inn which existed in his youth, run by the MacKellaigs, who live in the Mallaig area to this day. The inn was an incredible business before Mallaig replaced Tarbert as the main herring port. Donald had stories about herring barrels full of gold sovereigns being taken from the inn, over the hills under armed escort to meet the train in Arisaig.

Tarbert is blessed with a natural deep water harbour, which in Donald's younger days was filled with hundreds of drifters, and the pier head itself was a heaving throng of salting and curing, with accents and strange languages from as far afield as Russia. It is impossible to look on Tarbert bay now without thinking of what it must have been like in its heyday.

Not long after I came to Mallaig, I was approached by the local police sergeant, which had me racking my brains trying to remember what I had done wrong. "Oh, you're fine, Ewen," said the sergeant, "You haven't done anything wrong". "I was just wondering if you would mind taking a billy goat up to Donald Tarbert in your boat."

"Indeed I would," says I, as the nerves were still a wee bit shot after a heavy session. You see, this was no ordinary goat. It had escaped from Tarbert, and had come over the hill to Morar, where it had waged war on the gardens of local residents, who were not best pleased. I was pretty sure that the goat and I would not make particularly good shipmates, and I never did find out how the police got him back to his rightful owner.

It was probably not long afterwards that I got a call from the Council, asking if I would take a team of electricians to Tarbert, as the decision had been taken to connect Donald to the national grid, quite something when you consider that this was in the mid 1980s. Donald's sister Jessie thought it was a miracle when they switched the light on for the first time.

Which brings to mind the story of a man living in Arisaig when electric light first came to the area. Apparently he went to his bed, and his wife, who was in the next room, could hear

141

him blowing and blowing and blowing for all he was worth. When she knocked on the door and asked what on earth he was doing, he told her that he was trying to blow the light out.

It is still very difficult to get any kind of radio signal at Tarbert, although VHF was obtained by placing an aerial in a direct line from that of the Morrisons in Inverie; working on the principal that 'what you can see, you can hear.' Pretty rough and ready measurements, but effective never the less.

In fact, just a year or two ago, I ran aground in Loch Nevis and tried to contact the coast guard on the VHF to no avail. Eventually I managed to contact Inverie and they were able to send a boat out to rescue me.

Loch Nevis has a couple of celebrity residents these days, showbiz impresario Sir Cameron MacIntosh for one, and Tom 'Moby' Maclean, who has appeared in the Guinness Book of Records a number of times for his rowing exploits amongst other things. He once spent three weeks on Rockall, to try and claim it for the British government, and was ferried to and from the 'island' by Donald Patience or 'Donald the Vision' as he was known in Mallaig.

Donald was from Avoch on the Black Isle, and used to write the most wonderful letters into the Fishing News, which tended to be political, because, as we all know, fishing is in a constant turmoil, especially these days. Thousands of tons of cod being dumped and millions starving in the world. It's ridiculous.

Anyway, that is another story. Tom MacLean's achievements are there for all to see. He is a man who, I'm sure, had a tough upbringing, but carved out a career for himself in the army, and went onto serve with the SAS. He has a lovely wife, and his two sons were given the best education that money can buy when they went to Gordonstoun. Yes, he can be very proud.

I remember a few years ago, Sir Cameron MacIntosh handed out complimentary tickets to various local people for his stage show 'Les Miserables', and I was a wee bit annoyed that I wasn't given one. So, when I met one of the lucky people who had been to the show, I told them that, rather than looking 'les miserables', they looked 'more miserables' than they had beforehand.

Tex Geddes was another man to whom I could devote a whole book. Tex lived on the Island of Soay, and was a kenspeckle figure around Mallaig for many years. Tex was mentioned many times in Gavin Maxwell's publications, and no wonder. He came from the East Coast originally, possibly Morayshire, and settled in Soay just before the second war. He is probably best known as a shark fisherman.

When I first arrived in Mallaig, Tex had a young girl from England working with him on his boat, which I have to admit I found quite strange. Nobody had ever heard of this before. My word she was a capable girl though, and that was Tex, always something different.

I suppose, again, we were boozing buddies, and would sit together in the pub; one trying to out bullshit the other. We would often end up in Duncan Gillies' house, and that's when the contest would really start. One would be telling the other one to 'shut up and listen'. The thing about Tex was that although he boasted a lot, he had actually done most of the things that he boasted about.

All of the above would have been of great interest to an incredible woman whom I had the pleasure of meeting on many occasions, Margaret Fay Shaw, or as we knew her in Mallaig, Mrs. Campbell, Canna. She was one of the foremost collectors and archivists of folklore and folk culture in the world and lived to be over a hundred.

Hers was an amazing life story, and a lesson to us all. She came from the Alleghenies, near Pittsburgh, Pennsylvania and arrived in the Hebrides in 1929, where five years later she would meet her future husband John Lorne Campbell. Together they collected reams of archive material from all

143

over the Hebrides and beyond, which has gone a long way to safe guarding our culture for future generations. After buying the island of Canna in 1938, they made this their home and the base for their studies for over sixty years.

I have a photo of herself and I that was taken in the MacIntosh Centre in Mallaig while she was convalescing a few years ago. She was a very small woman with a huge personality and, of course, in the photo she's puffing away on the inevitable cigarette, which was never too far away from her. As she said herself "there's no point in stopping now." She donated a lovely piano to the centre, which is there yet, and anyone is free to play if they so wish.

She wrote many books, one of which, 'The Folklore of South Uist', has become incredibly important as a record of crofting life in the Hebrides during the 1930s. It covers all facets of the culture from old recipes to Gaelic waulking songs. She also made time to write a nice book about herself called 'From the Alleghenies to the Hebrides', which explains how she left her home in America to make a new life on South Uist, and how she met and befriended the MacRae sisters, who were to become amongst her most important imformants. They took her into their home and into their hearts and taught her the Gaelic.

She was a wonderful woman, and she smiled at me one day when I told her that although her husband had written many books, they were too academic for me, and I preferred her own.

Mr Campbell himself was a very learned man, who became very fluent in Gaelic, and many other languages, I believe. He had a very dry sense of humour, and on being asked one day by someone if he belonged to Canna, he replied, "No, Canna belongs to me."

They were an amazing couple, and have left, as part of their legacy, one of the most fantastic Gaelic libraries in the world, which, like the island of Canna, has been left to the care of the National Trust.

As I said before, I loved Glasgow. The city definitely did something for me. It intrigued me, as I suppose it was so different from the life I had known on Grimsay. During periods of leave, I would take any odd jobs that were going, just to keep me in Glasgow. I remember once taking a job as a deck hand on one of the many tug-boats that plied their trade up and down the river Clyde at that time. She was a terribly smelly, flea-ridden vessel and I didn't fancy living aboard, so, as often as not, I used to stay with an old cousin of mine in Govan.

Donald MacAulay lived with his wife and family in a single end in Burndike Street, and when I say single end, I mean single end. They showed me every hospitality though, and couldn't have done more for me during my stays there. They were very short of space, so old Donald and I used to have to share a bed, and because they only had two rooms, we had to work a rota where either the men got up first or the women got up first.

One morning in particular, Donald produced two boiled eggs, which were very brown indeed. When I asked him why they were so brown, he explained that he had made the tea and the eggs in the one pot. I said that I hoped he had cleaned the eggs first, to which Donald replied, "Och well, if they weren't clean, the tea would have cleaned them for me."

Donald's wife was an amazing woman, who often had to feed her grandchildren as well, as their daughters had married lazy men, who weren't into providing for their families. Poor Mrs MacAulay was worked off her feet, and there was always a pot of soup on the go in case any of her little urchins needed fed.

I also have family connections to other colourful characters, possibly the strangest being my connection to Hercules the bear.

You may well recall Hercules the bear and his disappearance on Benbecula in 1980. Well I have my own take on the story, as I was there, and Andy Robin is married to a cousin of mine from Grimsay.

Andy was the owner of Hercules, and was a bit of a bear himself (although a nice bear). He had been a champion wrestler and used to cut about Mallaig, Mull and Loch Sunart in this very fast 'Spear Fish' speedboat that he used to have. I remember my mother and my sister and I being up at his place in Glen Devon once, and he showed me the speedboat, which was extremely fast. He told me that he had ripped out the 300hp engine and replaced it with a 600hp model, which was fairly impressive, when you consider that the man didn't know much about navigation and so on. He just used to point the boat in the general direction he was going and he seemed to get on alright.

Him and his wife owned the Sheriffmuir Inn, and the bear would appear behind the bar, although, as I suggested earlier, when Andy was there you had to wonder which was which.

He became famous and, I suppose, made his fortune as the owner of Hercules, whom he got as a cub from Kincraig Wildlife Park, in Inverness-shire.

In 1980, Hercules would have been about 55 to 60 stone in weight; a huge beast, and Andy would wrestle with him in public, which soon attracted the attentions of the television cameras who knew when they were onto a good thing. Soon enough, he had attracted a number of different companies keen to enter into sponsorship deals (the best known of these being the television advertising campaign with Kleenex).

I believe Andy was in Uist filming a TV commercial with 'Big Herc', as he called him, or maybe his wife just liked the idea of taking the bear back to her ancestral home.

Anyway, Andy took the bear over to Petersport and then let him swim across to Wiay, a once inhabited island off the

146

east side, which had been the home of a fishing family by the name of MacRae, who still ply their trade in the Uists.

I'm not quite sure whether Andy expected him to swim straight back, but Hercules had other plans, and went missing for nearly three weeks. Poor Andy, in all fairness, was demented, and I can understand that. If anything were to happen to 'Jimmy the Cat' I would be inconsolable too. Plus the fact that Hercules meant a lot of money to Andy Robin.

Everyone was out looking for him; the army, the navy, you name it. There was even a thousand pound reward for a positive sighting, which was very attractive to a man so far gone with drink as I was at that stage. In fact, I felt very important out looking for the bear, puffing away on my cigarettes. I even hired my uncle's boat and took Andy round the coastline looking for 'Big Herc,'. I am not quite sure what I would have done if I had seen him, especially tramping across the moor, as these things can travel up to about thirty miles per hour. I'm not quite sure what the plan was, but you were never that far away from the next person, and plenty were armed just in case.

There was a lot of nonsense talked as well though, with reports of sheep being killed, and whole flocks disappearing in South Uist. I suppose, as with most things, there may have been an element of truth, but it definitely suited the papers to keep things sensational.

The bear was eventually spotted by a man from near Tigh a' Ghearraidh. He didn't have phone in his house and so asked his nearest neighbour for shot of his. His neighbour wasn't so daft. He told him that, yes, he could use the phone, but it would cost him £500; half the reward money

A Safe Mooring at Last

Mallaig has seen millions of pounds worth of development since I first came here; new roads, new houses and a new school. There has even been a new pier built, which wasn't to everyone's taste but still it was built.

I suppose I was one of the dissenting voices at the time. I felt the developers hadn't listened enough to the wishes or even the concerns of the local people. It's all very well testing things in a flume tank down in Hull, but there is really no substitute for local knowledge. As an old gentlemen, Charlie Henderson, from Mallaig said, "It's a pity they didn't consult some of the older types." It was a difficult job anyway, what with the depths of water involved, and the meeting of three different currents, but the refusal to act on any of the local advice offered just added to the problems.

The changes have been tremendous though and the only thing that I see wrong now is with the old folks' housing which has been recently built in the village. I heard rumours which, sure enough, proved to be true, that the main part of the houses look onto the side of a hill. Why couldn't they look out to sea where you could see something?

I had put my name down for one of these houses, but I just can't see myself living there now, especially when I have such a wonderful panoramic view from my tenement flat in Gillies Park at the moment. Another problem is that they have stairs, which I'm sure will cause problems for residents. I'm pretty lucky, I'm fit and healthy, but what of those who are possibly more infirm? They are almost three quarters finished now, and no one can deny that they are beautifully built, but why should they look onto the side of a hill? It is beyond me.

I suppose I was twenty-five years younger when I first came here, but it did seem to me that there was more comradeship, certainly in the pubs. Maybe times were better. Certainly the fishing was in a much healthier state. The whole industry now is so full of rules and regulations from Brussels. The paper work is horrendous, and there is no longer much of an incentive for young people to buy a new boat, because tomorrow is not guaranteed.

Being a Jehovah's Witness, I don't go in much for politics, but I have bought the Fishing News faithfully for the last twenty years, and am constantly amazed by some of the things I read. Fishermen on the East Coast who have so much money, and others have swimming pools. They have obviously worked very hard to get there, but this must also be over fishing, and that can't be helping. We blame the EU and all that but some of the time, the blame lies with ourselves. Fishermen can be their own worst enemy at times; "We'll go for this today, never mind about tomorrow."

There has been a steady decline in fishing in Mallaig, affecting the four main strands of the industry locally; trawling, purse netting, dredging and creel fishing. If you are determined to keep going, you can still make a living, but it has become increasingly difficult if you don't have some sort of financial backing. There is also now so much paper work to be filled in that going to sea actually becomes a secondary concern.

There are examples of families on the east coast in ports like Fraserburgh and Peterhead who have diversified into fish production, so that they are controlling every inch of the process from catching the fish, to getting the product to the supermarkets. But they looked after their money in the first place, in order to be able to do that. It is sad to say, but I suppose they were hungrier for success than us west coasters, who tend to be a bit more laid back. I certainly don't know of any fisherman on the west coast that has a swimming pool in their house.

They still seem to be doing well at the fishing in Ireland, but then, they were always hard workers as well. Shetland also seems to be enjoying better times, but here on the west coast, things are hard. The fun has gone out of the fishing locally. At one time you didn't even need to work particularly hard and were still assured of a good living, but those times are long gone. I even notice it walking down the pier. You don't get the same jokes or crack. Life has become a very serious business.

It is a very hard life, and I'm especially thinking of young guys, not even half my age. They'll be away at three in the morning, they have a young family, and they won't be back until nine at night, whereupon they are nearly falling asleep in their soup, with the result that the wee children don't know their dads.

Okay, they make money, but at a cost, because little children really should get quality time from their parents. That, of course, is my opinion, even though I was never married. I love children though, and love taking them out on my boat. Only today I was speaking to this wee girl, and her mother said, "You're lucky. She even spoke, and now she is telling you a story. You must have a gift for children." I suppose there is often a connection between young children and older people.

Mallaig, though, is no better or worse than any other place in the Highlands. People seem to be so busy, and television takes up so much of their time, and you are really not supposed to call on someone these days unless you have phoned or have an appointment. People are in such a rush. I know even my relations in Uist; 'Don't phone when Coronation Street is on', and if you do phone, you won't get a reply. I miss being able to call on people, and the ceilidhs of my youth, but we are living in a different world.

Even this very night, my sister said to me, "I wish to goodness I'd listened more to my mother. I could hear a voice, but I wasn't hearing the message." Sometimes we do that when people are talking. I know I'm very guilty of it.

Ironically though, moving to Mallaig has been a good thing for me, because I was able to change my life drastically with the help of the Alcoholics Anonymous and the Jehovah's Witnesses. I have been lucky. I enjoy my life now, but in another few months I'll be seventy-three years old, and other considerations appear on the horizon. I will eventually become too old to take the boat to sea, and that will be a wrench when it comes, but I am settled at last. Some days, depending on my mental state (or the weather) it can be hard, and at the moment she is out of the water, sitting high and dry on the pier while I carry out some repairs on her. The boat like myself is getting on.

It's funny though, I met a couple of men today, whom I think I have coaxed into coming up next summer. I gave them a business card, and they were able to have a look at the 'Grimsay Isle', so I must still have the urge somewhere. I even saw a couple down on the pier the other day, so I sidled up to them and said, "Ah, tourists. An unknown commodity at this time of year!" That broke the ice, and now they are coming back next year also.

I still love meeting people. You never know who or what the next day will bring, and I look forward to my repeat business, who become old friends rather than clients. I keep abreast of all the latest developments, and am currently having my website changed, which is quite a statement for a septuagenarian fisherman from North Uist. My advertising posters have, themselves, developed quite a cult following. They include pictures of Jimmy the cat and Annabel the seal, and I plan to add a picture of Scar Face the otter, the friend of the local fishing fleet. They also bear the legend 'GAELIC SPOKEN AT NO EXTRA COST. ENGLISH ATTEMPTED IF NECESSARY.'

I have a feeling that in the next ten to twenty years, marinas will become increasingly important around here, with a rise in the number of charter vessels, although it will be too late for me to worry about competition.

I would be quite happy to sell my business tomorrow, but only if whoever buys it would employ me in my normal capacity as skipper. They could easily put a young fellow aboard with me, and I could show him the ropes until it is my time to call it a day. After all, you pick up a few things in fifty odd years at sea. I seem to have a knack for talking with people, so maybe I would prove a good tutor.

I am happy where I am. Just last week I turned down one of the new council houses that have been built in Mallaig. The main living room looked onto the side of a hill, and I certainly wouldn't want that. I would miss my sea view. I wouldn't have been allowed an open fire, and there was no cat flap for Jimmy the cat, so that was the end of that. I toyed with the idea of moving to the island of Lewis, where they have a fairly healthy congregation of thirty or forty, but no, Mallaig has been good to me, and I think I'll stay.